ROUTES THROUGH ENGLISH

Andrew Bennett

Authors
in their Times

Comparative Readings
in GCSE English

Pearson Education Limited
Edinburgh Gate
Harlow
Essex
CM20 2JE

England and Associated Companies throughout the World

© Pearson Education Limited 1999

The right of Andrew Bennett to be identified as the author of this Work has been asserted by him in accordance with the Copyright, Designs and Patents Act of 1988.

All rights reserved. No part of this publication may be reproduced, stored in a retrieval system, or transmitted in any form or by any means, electronic, mechanical, photocopying, recording, or otherwise without the prior written permission of the Publishers or a licence permitting restricted copying in the United Kingdom issued by the Copyright Licensing Agency Ltd, 90 Tottenham Court Road, London, W1P 9HE

ISBN 0-582-41988-3

First published 1999

Printed in Italy by G. Canale & C. S.p.A.

The Publisher's policy is to use paper manufactured from sustainable forests.

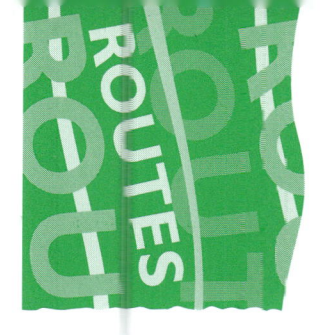

Contents

Introduction	**4**
1 Larger than life: 19th-century and 20th-century short stories	**8**
Mrs. Turner Cutting the Grass, Carol Shields (1994)	8
The Purple Pileus, H.G. Wells (1896)	15
2 Guilty consciences: genres from different periods	**29**
A Trampwoman's Tragedy, Thomas Hardy (1902)	31
Mr Policeman and the Cook, Wilkie Collins (1887)	35
A Confession Found in a Prison in the Time of Charles the Second, Charles Dickens (1840)	55
The Outside Dog, Alan Bennett (1998)	61
3 Staying or going: diverse texts	**74**
Silas Marner, George Eliot (1861) (extract)	75
Spoonface Steinberg, Lee Hall (1997) (extract)	83
4 Death or glory: texts on a theme	**88**
Fair Stood the Wind for France, H.E. Bates (1944) (extract)	89
To My Brother, Vera Brittain (1918)	93
Leave in 1917, Lilian M. Anderson (1930)	94
The Trumpet Major, Thomas Hardy (1880) (extract)	97
The Two Generals, Anthony Trollope (1863)	101
5 Only connect: making your own comparisons	**126**
6 Students' work: responses to comparative reading	**130**
Glossary of technical terms	**135**
Acknowledgements	**141**

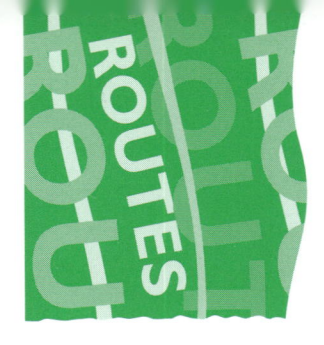

Introduction

Comparisons

We spend much of our lives making comparisons:

- which band do I prefer to hear?
- where can I eat the best burgers?
- who would play in my fantasy football team?
- which TV soap do I enjoy most?
- who is my closest friend?

Being able to explain our reasons is not always so easy.

It's no different when it comes to reading. At one time or another, most of us discover a book, or even just part of a book, which really speaks to us – writing which makes us understand **ideas**, feelings or **situations** in a way which we'd never thought of before.

Explaining that **impact** to someone else can be very difficult. One approach is by *comparing*: for example, the various ways writers treat a **theme**, create **characters** or use words to describe a situation. Comparing can help you identify just what it is that one writer does differently from another, and so what it is that appeals particularly to you, the reader.

In your GCSE courses, both English and English Literature, you must be able to show that you *can* explain how different writers achieve certain **effects** in you through *what* they write and *how* they write it. Sometimes you can do this through comparing texts which have obvious *similarities*; in their **subject-matter**, for example, or through what is known as the **genre** or **form** they take – such as **short stories**, poems, or playscripts. Sometimes, you can draw attention to the obvious *differences* between texts – for example, if they were written in different times or about different societies, or if the writers use a different **tone** (such as humorous or serious) in approaching their subject-matter or themes.

How will this book help me?

This book will help you make comparisons between texts. It includes a wide selection of complete texts and extracts, grouped in ways to make you think about their similarities and differences. This should help you decide which you prefer, and why. The texts come from different historical times; they are set in different societies, and are the work of a variety of writers. Some are short stories or extracts from longer **novels**, some are poems, and some are scripts written for radio or television performance.

To help you make judgements and form opinions, Chapters 1–4 include:

- texts selected around a theme
- ideas to help you think about each individual text and group of texts
- suggested written **tasks** on groups of texts

- glossaries of the meanings of difficult or unusual words in each text, arranged alphabetically.

In Chapter 6 you will find:

- general advice on planning **responses** to texts
- examples of tasks based on new groupings of texts in the book
- tasks which encourage you to include your own reading discoveries.

In Chapter 6 there are examples of students' writing which show the sort of responses you might aim for. At the end of the book there is a glossary of technical terms to help you understand and use the correct critical language in your own writing about texts. Technical terms explained in the glossary are printed in **bold** the first time they occur.

What skills do I need?

Before you start working on any of the texts, you need to know what GCSE examiners look for in your coursework **assignments** and examination answers. How do you show them that you are a skilful reader, someone who can express good ideas about what you have read, including judgements about the authors' **styles**, writing **techniques** and the effect they have on you, the reader?

The answer is, that you need to demonstrate certain **skills** which are common requirements of all GCSE **syllabuses**. The technical name for these skills is **assessment objectives**, and they require you to show that you have:

- understood what the writer is saying and are interested in it
- become involved with the themes, ideas, situations or characters written about
- been affected by reading the text, and can write about this effect in an appropriate way
- identified how the writer uses **language** and other techniques or skills to achieve those effects on you.

You also need to show that you can:

- make detailed **references** to texts, sometimes by describing general **features**, but also through using well-chosen **quotations**
- compare and make cross-references to aspects of texts where you can see connections of any kind, either similarities or differences
- recognise different ideas or suggestions in texts, perhaps beyond the **surface meaning** of the words or the situations.

You should also try to comment on:

- how language varies in different **societies** or **cultures** (for example, in the United Kingdom and North America)
- how language has changed over a period of time (for example, between the nineteenth and twentieth centuries)
- what difference these variations and changes make to your response
- how the society, culture or historical period in which a text is set influences the writer's ideas or **approach**, and how this affects your understanding of his or her **purpose**

- how writers use **literary conventions** (for example, **rhyme** in a poem or different viewpoints in a novel) to create particular effects, and whether they are appropriate to the subject-matter.

How do I obtain a good grade?

Even if you demonstrate all the skills listed above in your writing about texts, your GCSE grade will depend on how well you illustrate and develop each of them If you simply:

- show awareness of the most obvious features and meanings of texts, and
- make few detailed references,

you will not score better than a grade F. If you can:

- explain why you prefer one text to another
- begin to identify and compare precise details in each of them, and
- show you can see different ways of understanding them

then you have moved up into grade C territory. When you are also able to:

- analyse the effects of writers' techniques
- make your own informed judgements about the use they make of social or cultural references and of **literary traditions**, and
- suggest original ways of interpreting their work

you will gain the very highest grades.

How do I write about texts?

In each of Chapters 1–4 suggestions for responding to the texts are included. These are intended to set you thinking about them, and how you might write about them; you, or your teacher, may come up with other approaches which suit you better. That's fine – as long as you:

- remember to plan any task so that it gives you plenty of opportunity to cover the skills listed above, and
- check any particular requirements of the GCSE syllabus you are following.

If you enjoy a complete text in this book, try reading more by the same author; in the case of extracts, try reading either the whole text or other parts of it. As well as increasing the pleasure you get from reading, this will allow you to develop ideas for planning your own piece of work which compares texts, particularly if you want to follow up some of the suggestions in Chapter 5.

In Chapter 6, you will find examples of students' writing which briefly illustrate the skills you need to develop in comparing texts. Use these examples to think about how well your own writing gets over your understanding: is it as good as these examples, or better? How could it be improved?

Before you attempt even to plan the outline of a written response, discuss your ideas with your teacher, a friend or a parent – you may find it easier to sort out your first thoughts by talking them through, and any questions you are asked may help you **focus** your ideas more clearly. Remember to use the glossary at the end of this book if you are unsure about the meaning of any critical terms: it will improve your chances of a high grade if you understand and can use technical language correctly.

How do I get started?

The best way to approach this part of your GCSE course is to start by reading widely among the texts collected in this book. Although Chapters 1–4 are not arranged in order of difficulty, you will find it helpful to keep to the groupings within chapters at first, even if you read the chapters in a different order. Give all the texts a try – you may be surprised at what you enjoy. Don't be put off by texts written a long time ago, even if they seem to be written in a difficult style or feel rather slow-moving at first. Read the more challenging texts in short sections, pausing regularly to ask yourself questions such as:

- What makes it difficult to read? Is it particular aspects of the style or **structure**? Is it the subject-matter?
- Why did the author write this? What was his or her purpose?
- Am I getting new ideas or understanding from it?
- What do I like best about it so far?
- How do I think it may develop from this point? Why?

Jot down your responses to these questions and file them safely away – by the time you have read the whole of the text, you will have a useful set of notes around which you can plan a written, personal response at the right time. As you read more widely, you will begin to remember having similar feelings about other texts and so will be able to note points of comparison or contrast between them. Chapter 5 encourages you to look for your own connections between texts, so be prepared to take time in thinking carefully about what they mean to you and how you could best get across that understanding to someone else in a piece of written work.

If you really do not find a text sufficiently powerful or interesting to keep detailed notes about it, try at least to identify and remember aspects which you may be able to refer to when writing about other texts. These could be:

- a particular use of language
- the presentation of a character or a situation
- the use made of genre qualities.

And finally...

...this collection of texts should be seen as just a starting-point from which you can explore further to discover stories, poems and plays which give you a whole new outlook on life. Of course, you don't always have to analyse texts deeply to enjoy them but, if you learn some of the techniques and skills suggested here, they will soon become part of your natural response to texts when you read them for the first time. In turn, this will develop your ability to form and justify opinions, and it may even sharpen your own writing skills through being able to use some of the techniques you recognise in the work of professional authors.

Larger than life: 19th and 20th century short stories

Introduction

In this chapter, two complete short stories have been selected for you to study. The first, *Mrs. Turner Cutting the Grass*, is by the contemporary North American writer, Carol Shields. Published in 1994, it is set in modern-day Canada. The second story is by the British writer H.G. Wells; *The Purple Pileus* was published in 1895, one year after his well-known first novel, *The Time Machine*.

Both stories contain a strongly-presented central character, but include other characters whose **actions**, words and **attitudes** are vital in shaping your feelings about situations. In both stories, the authors themselves make direct comments about characters which significantly affect the way you think about them. In spite of this directness, and the fact that both stories are apparently funny or light-hearted, you can read some serious **messages** between the lines.

Reading the Carol Shields

As you read *Mrs. Turner Cutting the Grass*, think about the following issues.

- What are your first impressions of Mrs Turner? Do those first impressions change as you read further? If so, when and why?
- What do you feel about her neighbours' and the schoolgirls' attitudes to her?
- Is the professor-poet a totally unlikeable man?
- What does the author feel about her characters and what makes you think that?
- What are the serious themes in this story?

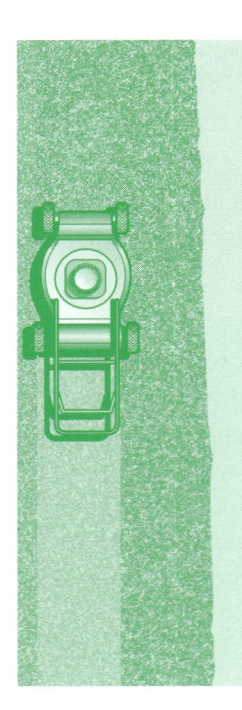

Mrs. Turner Cutting the Grass
by Carol Shields

Oh, Mrs. Turner is a sight cutting the grass on a hot afternoon in June! She climbs into an ancient pair of shorts and ties on her halter top and wedges her feet into crepe-soled sandals and covers her red-grey frizz with Gord's old golf cap – Gord is dead now, 10 years ago, a seizure on a Saturday night while winding the mantel clock.

The grass flies up around Mrs. Turner's knees. Why doesn't she use a catcher, the Saschers next door wonder. Everyone knows that leaving the clippings like that is bad for the lawn. Each fallen blade of grass throws a minute shadow which impedes growth and repair. The Saschers themselves use their clippings to make compost which they hope one day will be ripe as the good manure that Sally Sascher's father used to spread on his fields down near Emerson Township.

Mrs. Turner's carelessness over the clippings plucks away at Sally, but her husband Roy is far more concerned about the Killex that Mrs. Turner dumps on her dandelions. It's true that in Winnipeg the dandelion roots go right to the middle of the earth, but Roy is patient and persistent in pulling them out, knowing exactly how to grasp the coarse leaves in his hand and how much pressure to apply. Mostly they come up like corks with their roots intact. And he and Sally are experimenting with new ways to cook dandelion greens, believing as they do that the components of nature are arranged for a specific purpose – if only that purpose can be divined.

In the early summer Mrs. Turner is out every morning by 10 with her sprinkling can of chemical killer, and Roy, watching from his front porch, imagines how this poison will enter the ecosystem and move by quick capillary surges into his fenced vegetable plot, newly seeded now with green beans and lettuce. His children, his two little girls aged two and four – that they should be touched by such poison makes him morose and angry. But he and Sally so far have said nothing to Mrs. Turner about her abuse of the planet because they're hoping she'll go into an old-folks' home soon or maybe die, and then all will proceed as it should.

High-school girls on their way home in the afternoon see Mrs. Turner cutting her grass and are mildly, momentarily repelled by the lapped, striated flesh on her upper thighs. At her age. Doesn't she realise? Every last one of them is intimate with the vocabulary of skincare and knows that what has claimed Mrs. Turner's thighs is the enemy called cellulite, but they can't understand why she doesn't take the trouble to hide it. It makes them queasy; it makes them fear for the future.

The things Mrs. Turner doesn't know would fill the Saschers' new compost pit, would sink a ship, would set off a tidal wave, would make her want to kill herself. Back and forth, back and forth she goes with the electric lawn mower, the grass flying out sideways like whiskers. Oh, the things she doesn't know! She has never heard, for example, of the folk-rock recording star Neil Young, though the high school just around the corner from her house happens to be the very school Neil Young attended as a lad. His initials can actually be seen carved on one of the desks, and a few of the teachers say they remember him, a quiet fellow of neat appearance and always very polite in class. The desk with the initials NY is kept in a corner of Mr. Pring's homeroom, and it's considered lucky – despite the fact that the renowned singer wasn't a great scholar – to touch the incised letters just before an exam. Since it's exam time now, the second week of June, the girls walking past Mrs. Turner's front yard (and shuddering over her display of cellulite) are carrying on their fingertips the spiritual scent, the essence, the fragrance, the aura of Neil Young, but Mrs. Turner is as ignorant of that fact as the girls are that she, Mrs. Turner, possesses a first name – which is Geraldine.

Not that she's ever been called Geraldine. Where she grew up in Boissevain, Manitoba, she was known always – the Lord knows why – as Girlie Fergus, the youngest of the three Fergus girls and the one who got herself in hot water. Her sister Em went to normal school and her sister Muriel went to Brandon to work at Eatons, but Girlie got caught one night – she was 19 – in a Boissevain hotel room with a local farmer, married, named Gus MacGregor. It was her father who got wind of where she might be and came banging on the door, shouting and weeping, 'Girlie, Girlie, what have you done to me?'

Girlie had been working in the Boissevain Dairy since she'd left school at 16 and had a bit of money saved up, and so, a week after the humiliation in the local hotel, she wrote a farewell note to the family, crept out of the house at midnight and caught the bus to Winnipeg. From there she got another bus down to Minneapolis, then to Chicago and finally New York City. The journey was endless and wretched, and on the way across Indiana and Ohio and Pennsylvania she saw hundreds of towns whose unpaved streets and narrow, blinded houses made her fear some conspiratorial punishing power had carried her back to Boissevain. Her father's soppy-stern voice sang and sang in her ears as the wooden bus rattled its way eastward. It was summer, 1930.

New York was immense and wonderful, dirty, perilous and puzzling. She found herself longing for a sight of real earth which she assumed must lie somewhere beneath the tough pavement. On the other hand, the brown flat-roofed factories with their little windows tilted skywards pumped her full of happiness, as did the dusty trees, when she finally discovered them, lining the long avenues. Every last person in the world seemed to be outside walking, filling the streets, and every corner breezed with noise and sunlight. She had to pinch herself to believe this was the same sunlight that filtered its way into the rooms of the house back in Boissevain, fading the curtains but nourishing her mother's ferns. She sent postcards to Em and Muriel which said, 'Don't worry about me. I've got a job in the theatre business.'

It was true. For eight-and-a-half months she was an usherette in the Lamar Movie Palace in Brooklyn. She loved her perky maroon uniform, the way it fitted on her shoulders, the way the strips of crinkly, gold braid outlined her figure. With a little flashlight in hand she was able to send streams of light across the furry darkness of the theatre and on the plum-coloured aisle carpet. The voices from the screen talked on and on. She felt after a time that their resonant declarations and tender replies belonged to her.

She met a man named Kiki in her first month in New York and moved in with him. His skin was as black as ebony. *As black as ebony* – that was the phrase that hung like a ribbon on the end of his name, and it's also the phrase she uses, infrequently, when she wants to call up his memory, though she's more than a little doubtful about what *ebony* is. It may be a kind of stone, she thinks, something round and polished that comes out of a deep mine.

Kiki was a good-hearted man, though she didn't like the beer he drank, and he stayed with her, willingly for several months after she had to stop working because of the baby. It was the baby itself that frightened him off, the way it cried probably. Leaving 50 dollars on the table, he slipped out one July afternoon when Girlie was shopping, and went back to Troy, New York, where he'd been raised.

Her first thought was to take the baby and get on a bus and go find him, but there wasn't enough money, and the thought of the baby crying all the way on the hot bus made her feel tired. She was worried about the rent and about the little red sores in the baby's ear – it was a boy, rather sweetly formed, with wonderful smooth feet and hands. On a murderously hot night, a night when the humidity was especially bad, she wrapped him in a clean piece of sheeting and carried him all the way to Brooklyn Heights where the houses were large and solid and surrounded by grass. There was a house on a corner she particularly liked because it had a wide front porch (like those in Boissevain) with a curved railing – and parked on the porch, its brake on, was a beautiful wicker baby carriage. It was here she placed her baby, giving one last look to his sleeping face, as round and calm as the moon. She walked home, taking her time, swinging her legs. If she had known the word *foundling* – which she didn't – she would have bounded along on its rhythmic back, so airy and wide did the world seem that night.

Most of these secrets she keeps locked away inside her mottled thighs or in the curled pinkness of her genital flesh. She has no idea what happened to Kiki, whether he went off to Alaska as he wanted to or whether he fell down a flight of stone steps in the silverware factory in Troy, New York, and died of head injuries before his 30th birthday. Or what happened to her son – whether he was bitten that night in the baby carriage by a rabid cat or whether he was discovered the next morning and adopted by the large, loving family who lived in the house. As a rule, Girlie tries not to think about the things she can't even guess at. All she thinks is that she did the best she could under the circumstances.

In a year she saved enough money to take the train home to Boissevain. She took with her all her belongings, and also gifts for Em and Muriel, boxes of hose, bottles of apple blossom cologne, phonograph records. For her mother she took an embroidered apron and for her father a pipe made of curious gnarled wood, 'Girlie, my Girlie,' her father said, embracing her at the station. Then he said, 'Don't ever leave us again,' in a way that frightened her and made her resolve to leave as quickly as possible.

But she didn't go far the second time around. She and Gordon Turner – he was, for all his life, a tongue-tied man, though he did manage a proper proposal – settled down in Winnipeg, first in St. Boniface where the rents were cheap and then Fort Rouge and finally the little house in River Heights just around the corner from the high school. It was her husband Gord who planted the grass that Mrs. Turner now shaves in the summertime. It was Gord who trimmed and shaped the caragana hedge and Gord who painted the little shutters with the cut-out hearts. He was a man who loved every inch of his house, the wide wooden steps, the oak door with its glass inset, the radiators and the baseboards and the snug sash windows. And he loved every inch of his wife, Girlie, too, saying to her once, and only once, that he knew about her past (meaning Gus MacGregor and the incident in the Boissevain Hotel) and that as far as he was concerned the slate had been wiped clean. Once he came home with a little package in his pocket: inside was a diamond ring, delicate and glittering. Once he took Girlie on a picnic all the way up to Steep Rock, and in the woods he took off her dress and underthings and kissed every part of her body.

After he died, Girlie began to travel. She was far from rich, as she liked to say, but with care she could manage one trip every spring.

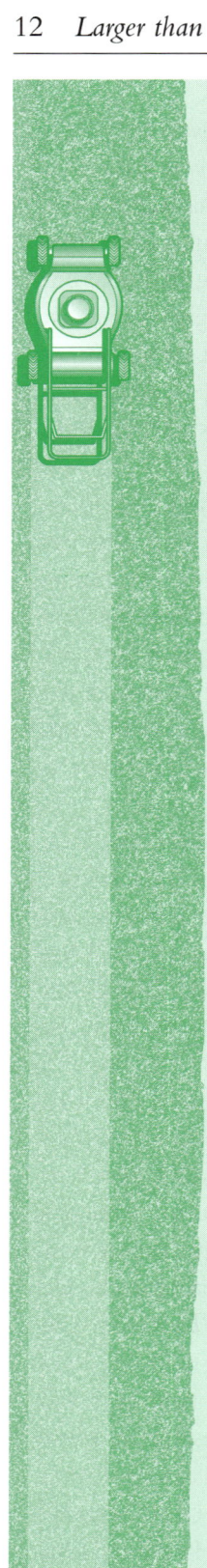

She has never known such ease. She and Em and Muriel have been to Disneyland as well as Disney World. They've been to Europe, taking a 16-day trip through seven countries. The three of them have visited the South and seen the famous antebellum houses of Georgia, Alabama and Mississippi, after which they spent a week in the city of New Orleans. They went to Mexico one year and took pictures of Mayan ruins and queer, shadowy gods cut squarely from stone. And three years ago they did what they swore they'd never have the nerve to do: they got on an airplane and went to Japan.

The package tour started in Tokyo where Mrs. Turner ate, on her first night there, a chrysanthemum fried in hot oil. She saw a village where everyone earned a living by making dolls and another village where everyone made pottery. Members of the tour group, each holding up a green flag so their tour leader could keep track of them, climbed on a little train, zoomed off to Osaka where they visited an electronics factory, and then went to a restaurant to eat uncooked fish. They visited more temples and shrines than Mrs. Turner could keep track of. Once they stayed the night in a Japanese hotel where she and Em and Muriel bedded down on floor mats and little pillows stuffed with cracked wheat, and woke up, laughing, with backaches and shooting pains in their legs. That was the same day they visited the Golden Pavilion in Kyoto. The three-storey temple was made of wood and had a roof like a set of wings and was painted a soft old flaky gold. Everybody in the group took pictures – Em took a whole roll – and bought postcards; everybody, that is, except a single tour member, the one they all referred to as the Professor. The Professor travelled without a camera, but jotted notes almost continuously into a little pocket scribbler. He was bald, had a trim body and wore Bermuda shorts, sandals and black nylon socks. Those who asked him learned that he really was a professor, a teacher of English poetry in a small college in Massachusetts. He was also a poet who, at the time of the Japanese trip, had published two small chapbooks based mainly on the breakdown of his marriage. The poems, sadly, had not caused much of a stir.

It grieved him to think of that paltry, guarded nut-like thing that was his artistic reputation. His domestic life had been too cluttered; there had been too many professional demands; the political situation in America had drained him of energy – these were the thoughts that buzzed in his skull as he scribbled and scribbled, like a man with a fever, in the back seat of a tour bus travelling through Japan.

Here in this crowded, confused country he discovered simplicity and order and something spiritual, too, which he recognised as being authentic. He felt as though a flower, something like a lily, only smaller and tougher, had unfurled in his hand and was nudging along his fountain pen. He wrote and wrote, shaken by catharsis, but lulled into a new sense of his powers.

Not surprisingly, a solid little book of poems came out of his experience. It was published soon afterwards by a well-thought-of Boston publisher who, as soon as possible, sent him around the United States to give poetry readings.

Mostly the Professor read his poems in universities and colleges where his book was already listed on the Contemporary Poetry course. He read in faculty clubs, student centres, classrooms, gymnasiums and auditoriums, and usually, part way through a reading someone or other would call from the back of the room, 'Give us your Golden Pavilion poem.'

He would have preferred to read his Fuji meditation or the tone poem of the Inner Sea, but he was happy to oblige his audiences, though he felt *A Day at the Golden Pavilion* was a somewhat light piece, even what is sometimes known on the circuit as a 'crowd pleaser'. People (admittedly they were mostly undergraduates) laughed out loud when they heard it; he read it well, too, in a moist, avuncular, amateur actor's voice, reminding himself to pause frequently, to look upwards and raise an ironic eyebrow. The poem was not really about the Golden Pavilion at all, but about three Midwestern lady tourists who, while viewing the temple and madly snapping photos, had talked incessantly and in loud, flat-bottomed voices about knitting patterns, indigestion, sore feet, breast lumps, the cost of plastic raincoats and a previous trip they'd made together to Mexico. They had wondered, these three – noisily, repeatedly – who back home in Manitoba should receive a postcard, what they'd give for an honest cup of tea, if there was an easy way to remove stains from an electric coffee maker, and where they would go the following year, Hawaii? They were the three Furies, the three witches, who for vulgarity and tastelessness formed a shattering counterpoint to the Professor's own state of transcendence. He had been affronted, angered, half-crazed.

One of the sisters, a little pug of a woman, particularly stirred his contempt, she of the pink pantsuit, the red toenails, the grapefruity buttocks, the overly bright souvenirs, the garish Mexican straw bag containing Dentyne chewing gum, aspirin, breath mints, sun goggles, envelopes of saccharine, and photos of her dead husband standing in front of a squat, ugly house in Winnipeg. This defilement she had spread before the ancient and exquisitely proportioned Golden Pavilion of Kyoto, proving – and here the Professor's tone became grave – proving that sublime beauty can be brought to the very doorway of human eyes, ears and lips and remain unperceived. When he comes to the end of *A Day at the Golden Pavilion* there is generally a thoughtful half-second of silence, then laughter and applause. Students turn in their seats and exchange looks with their fellows. They have seen such unspeakable tourists themselves. There was old Auntie Marigold or Auntie Flossie. There was that tacky Mrs. Shannon with her rouge and her jewellery. They know – despite their youth, they know – the irreconcilable distance between taste and banality. Or perhaps that's too harsh; perhaps it's only the difference between those who know about the world and those who don't.

It's true Mrs. Turner remembers little about her travels. She's never had much of a head for history or dates; she never did learn, for instance, the difference between a Buddhist temple and a Shinto shrine. She gets on a tour bus and goes and goes, and that's all there is to it. She doesn't know if she's going north or south or east or west. What does it matter? She's having a grand time. And she's reassured, always, by the sameness of the world. She's never heard the word *commonality*, but is nevertheless fused with its sense. In Japan she was made as happy to see carrots and lettuce growing in the fields as she was to see sunlight, years earlier, pouring into the streets of New York City. Everywhere she's been she's seen people eating and sleeping and working and making things with their hands and urging things to grow. There have been cats and dogs, fences and bicycles and telephone poles, and objects to buy and take care of; it is amazing, she thinks, that she can understand so much of the world and that it comes to her as easily as bars of music floating out of a radio.

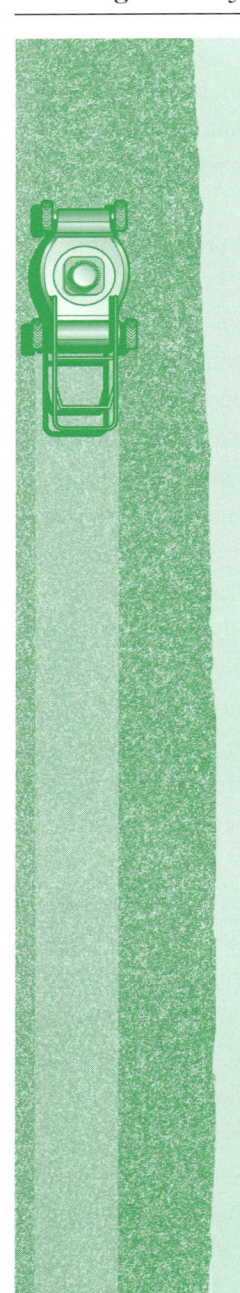

Her sisters have long forgotten about her wild days. Now the three of them love to sit on tour buses and chatter away about old friends and family members, their stern father and their mother who never once took their part against him. Muriel carries on about her children (a son in California and a daughter in Toronto) and she brings along snaps of her grandchildren to pass round. Em has retired from school teaching and is a volunteer in the Boissevain Local History Museum, to which she had donated several family mementos; her father's old carved pipe and her mother's wedding veil and, in a separate case, for all the world to see, a white cotton garment labelled 'Girlie Fergus Underdrawers, handmade, trimmed with lace, circa 1918'. If Mrs. Turner knew the word irony she would relish this. Even without knowing the word irony, she relishes it.

The professor from Massachusetts has won an important international award for his books of poems; translation rights have been sold to a number of foreign publishers; and recently his picture appeared in *The New York Times*, along with a lengthy quotation from *A Day at the Golden Pavilion*. How providential, some will think, that Mrs. Turner doesn't read *The New York Times* or attend poetry readings, for it might injure her deeply to know how she appears in certain people's eyes, but then there are so many things she doesn't know.

In the summer, as she cuts the grass, to and fro, to and fro, she waves to everyone she sees. She waves to the high-school girls who timidly wave back. She hollers hello to Sally and Roy Sascher and asks them how their garden is coming on. She cannot imagine that anyone would wish her harm. All she's done is live her life. The green grass flies up in the air, a buoyant cloud swirling about her head. Oh, what a sight is Mrs. Turner cutting her grass and how, like an ornament, she shines.

Reading the H.G. Wells

H.G. Wells' story differs from *Mrs. Turner Cutting the Grass* in many obvious ways: it was written almost one hundred years earlier and is set in England; the central character is a man, and the story was written by a man. It describes in some detail one episode in the life of Jim Coombes, rather than ranging over most of a life as happened with Mrs Turner.

Yet there are similarities, too. The central character is looked down upon by other characters, but in the end achieves a kind of contentment; and while it is (on the surface) a comic story, you could argue that there are serious underlying themes.

As you read *The Purple Pileus*, think about the following issues.

- Does the author appear to like *any* of the characters in the story?
- Are the female characters portrayed more harshly than the men?
- In what different ways does the **comedy** come from description, speech, situation and action?
- What are some of the serious themes underlying this story?
- How is it helpful to know when this story was written?

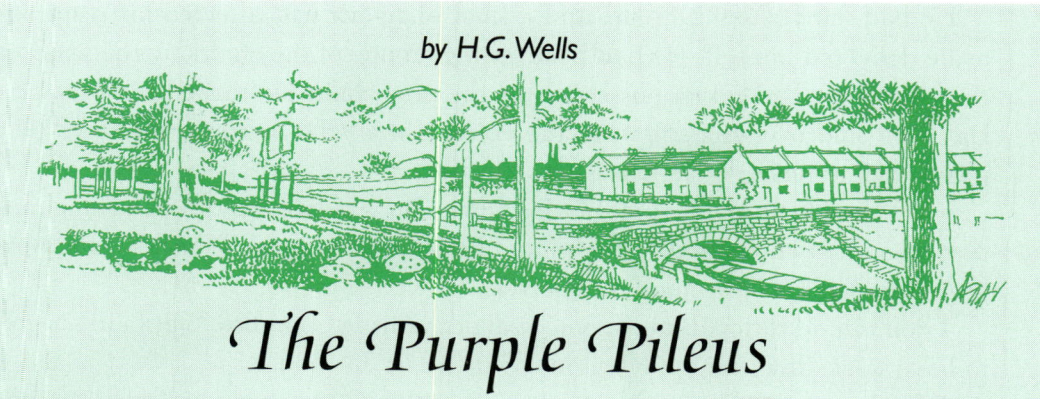

by H.G. Wells

The Purple Pileus

Mr Coombes was sick of life. He walked away from his unhappy home, and, sick not only of his own existence but of everybody else's, turned aside down Gaswork Lane to avoid the town, and, crossing the wooden bridge that goes over the canal to Starling's Cottages, was presently alone in the damp pine woods and out of sight and sound of human habitation. He would stand it no longer. He repeated aloud with blasphemies unusual to him that he would stand it no longer.

He was a pale-faced little man, with dark eyes and a fine and very black moustache. He had a very stiff, upright collar slightly frayed, that gave him an illusory double chin, and his overcoat (albeit shabby) was trimmed with astrachan. His gloves were a bright brown with black stripes over the knuckles, and split at the finger ends. His appearance, his wife had said once in the dear, dead days beyond recall – before he married her, that is – was military. But now she called him – it seems a dreadful thing to tell of between husband and wife, but she called him 'a little grub'. It wasn't the only thing she had called him, either.

The row had arisen about that beastly Jennie again. Jennie was his wife's friend, and, by no invitation of Mr Coombes, she came in every blessed Sunday to dinner, and made a shindy all the afternoon. She was a big, noisy girl, with a taste for loud colours and a strident laugh; and this Sunday she had outdone all her previous intrusions by bringing in a fellow with her, a chap as showy as herself. And Mr Coombes, in a starchy, clean collar and his Sunday frock-coat, had sat dumb and wrathful at his own table, while his wife and her guests talked foolishly and undesirably, and laughed aloud. Well, he stood that, and after dinner (which, 'as usual', was late), what must Miss Jennie do but go to the piano and play banjo tunes, for all the world as if it were a week-day! Flesh and blood could not endure such goings on. They would hear next door, they would hear in the road, it was a public announcement of their disrepute. He had to speak.

He had felt himself go pale, and a kind of rigour had affected his respiration as he delivered himself. He had been sitting on one of the chairs by the window – the new guest had taken possession of the arm-chair. He turned his head. 'Sun Day!' he said over the collar, in the voice of one who warns. 'Sun Day!' What people call a 'nasty' tone, it was.

Jennie had kept on playing, but his wife, who was looking through some music that was piled on the top of the piano, had stared at him. 'What's wrong now?' she said; 'can't people enjoy themselves?'

'I don't mind rational 'njoyment, at all.' said little Coombes, 'but I ain't a-going to have week-day tunes playing on a Sunday in this house.'

'What's wrong with my playing now?' said Jennie, stopping and twirling round on the music-stool with a monstrous rustle of flounces.

Coombes saw it was going to be a row, and opened too vigorously, as is common with your timid, nervous men all the world over. 'Steady on with that music-stool!' said he; 'it ain't made for 'eavy-weights.'

'Never you mind about weights,' said Jennie, incensed. 'What was you saying behind my back about my playing?'

'Surely you don't 'old with not having a bit of music on a Sunday, Mr Coombes?' said the new guest, leaning back in the arm-chair, blowing a cloud of cigarette smoke and smiling in a kind of pitying way. And simultaneously his wife said something to Jennie about 'Never mind 'im. You go on, Jinny.'

'I do,' said Mr Coombes, addressing the new guest.

'May I arst why?' said the new guest, evidently enjoying both his cigarette and the prospect of an argument. He was, by-the-by, a lank young man, very stylishly dressed in bright drab, with a white cravat and a pearl and silver pin. It had been better taste to come in a black coat, Mr Coombes thought.

'Because,' began Mr Coombes, 'it don't suit me. I'm a business man. I 'ave to study my connection. Rational 'njoyment—'

'His connection!' said Mrs Coombes scornfully. 'That's what he's always a-saying. We got to do this, and we got to do that—'

'If you don't mean to study my connection,' said Mr Coombes, 'what did you marry me for.'

'I wonder,' said Jennie, and turned back to the piano.

'I never saw such a man as you,' said Mrs Coombes. 'You've altered all round since we were married. Before—'

Then Jennie began at the tum, tum, tum again.

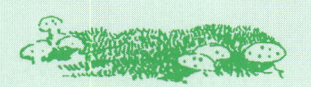

'Look here!' said Mr Coombes, driven at last to revolt, standing up and raising his voice. 'I tell you I won't have that.' The frock-coat heaved with his indignation.

'No vi'lence, now,' said the long young man in drab, sitting up.

'Who the juice are you?' said Mr Coombes fiercely.

Whereupon they all began talking at once. The new guest said he was Jennie's 'intended', and meant to protect her, and Mr Coombes said he was welcome to do so anywhere but in his (Mr Coombes') house; and Mrs Coombes said he ought to be ashamed of insulting his guests, and (as I have already mentioned) that he was getting a regular little grub; and the end was, that Mr Coombes ordered his visitors out of the house, and they wouldn't go, and so he said he would go himself. With his face burning and tears of excitement in his eyes, he went into the passage, and as he struggled with his overcoat – his frock-coat sleeves got concertinaed up his arm – and gave a brush at his silk hat, Jennie began again at the piano, and strummed him insultingly out of the house. Tum, tum, tum. He slammed the shop door so that the house quivered. That, briefly, was the immediate making of his mood. You will perhaps begin to understand his disgust with existence.

As he walked along the muddy path under the firs, – it was late October, and the ditches and heaps of fir needles were gorgeous with clumps of fungi, – he recapitulated the melancholy history of his marriage. It was brief and commonplace enough. He now perceived with sufficient clearness that his wife had married him out of a natural curiosity and in order to escape from her worrying, laborious, and uncertain life in the workroom; and, like the majority of her class, she was far too stupid to realise that it was her duty to co-operate with him in his business. She was greedy of enjoyment, loquacious, and socially-minded, and evidently disappointed to find the restraints of poverty still hanging about her. His worries exasperated her, and the slightest attempt to control her proceedings resulted in a charge of 'grumbling'. Why couldn't he be nice – as he used to be? And Coombes was such a harmless little man, too, nourished mentally on *Self-Help*, and with a meagre ambition of self-denial and competition, that was to end in a 'sufficiency'. Then Jennie came in as a female Mephistopheles, a gabbling chronicle of 'fellers', and was always wanting his wife to go to theatres, and 'all that'. And in addition were aunts of his wife, and cousins (male and female) to eat up capital, insult him personally, upset business arrangements, annoy good customers, and generally blight his life. It was not the first occasion by many that Mr Coombes had fled his home in wrath and indignation, and something like fear, vowing furiously and even aloud that he wouldn't stand it, and so frothing away his energy along the line of least resistance. But never before had he been quite so sick of life as on this particular Sunday afternoon. The Sunday dinner may have had its share in his despair – and the greyness of the sky. Perhaps, too, he was beginning to realise his unendurable frustration as a business man as the consequence of his marriage. Presently bankruptcy, and after that – Perhaps she might have reason to repent when it was too late. And destiny, as I have already intimated, had planted the path through the wood with evil-smelling fungi, thickly and variously planted it, not only on the right side, but on the left.

A small shopman is in such a melancholy position, if his wife turns out a disloyal partner. His capital is all tied up in his business, and to leave her means to join the unemployed in some strange part of the earth. The luxuries of divorce are beyond him altogether. So that the good old tradition of marriage for better or worse holds inexorably for him, and things work up to tragic culminations. Bricklayers kick their wives to death, and dukes betray theirs; but it is among the small clerks and shopkeepers nowadays that it comes most often to a cutting of throats. Under the circumstances it is not so very remarkable – and you must take it as charitably as you can – that the mind of Mr Coombes ran for a while on some such glorious close to his disappointed hopes, and that he thought of razors, pistols, bread-knives, and touching letters to the coroner denouncing his enemies by name, and praying piously for forgiveness. After a time his fierceness gave way to melancholia. He had been married in this very overcoat, in his first and only frock-coat that was buttoned up beneath it. He began to recall their courting along this very walk, his years of penurious saving to get capital, and the bright hopefulness of his marrying days. For it all to work out like this! Was there no sympathetic ruler anywhere in the world? He reverted to death as a topic.

He thought of the canal he had just crossed, and doubted whether he shouldn't stand with his head out, even in the middle, and it was while drowning was in his mind that the purple pileus caught his eye. He looked at it mechanically for a moment, and stopped and stooped towards it to pick it up, under the impression that it was some such small leather object as a purse. Then he saw that it was the purple top of a fungus, a peculiarly poisonous-looking purple: slimy, shiny, and emitting a sour odour. He hesitated with his hand an inch or so from it, and the thought of poison crossed his mind. With that he picked the thing, and stood up again with it in his hand.

The odour was certainly strong – acrid, but by no means disgusting. He broke off a piece, and the fresh surface was a creamy white, that changed like magic in the space of ten seconds to a yellowish-green colour. It was even an inviting-looking change. He broke off two other pieces to see it repeated. They were wonderful things these fungi, thought Mr Coombes, and all of them the deadliest poisons, as his father had often told him. Deadly poisons!

There is no time like the present for a rash resolve. Why not here and now? thought Mr Coombes. He tasted a little piece, a very little piece indeed – a mere crumb. It was so pungent that he almost spat it out again, then merely hot and full-flavoured: a kind of German mustard with a touch of horse-radish and – well, mushroom. He swallowed it in the excitement of the moment. Did he like it or did he not? His mind was curiously careless. He would try another bit. It really wasn't bad – it was good. He forgot his troubles in the interest of the immediate moment. Playing with death it was. He took another bite, and then deliberately finished a mouthful. A curious, tingling sensation began in his finger-tips and toes. His pulse began to move faster. The blood in his ears sounded like a mill-race. 'Try bi' more,' said Mr Coombes. He turned and looked about him, and found his feet unsteady. He saw, and struggled towards, a little patch of purple a dozen yards away. 'Jol' goo' stuff,' said Mr Coombes. 'E – lomore ye'.' He pitched forward and fell on his face, his hands outstretched towards the cluster of pilei. But he did not eat any more of them. He forgot forthwith.

He rolled over and sat up with a look of astonishment on his face. His carefully brushed silk hat had rolled away towards the ditch. He pressed his hand to his brow. Something had happened, but he could not rightly determine what it was. Anyhow, he was no longer dull – he felt bright, cheerful. And his throat was afire. He laughed in the sudden gaiety of his heart. Had he been dull? He did not know; but at anyrate he would be dull no longer. He got up and stood unsteadily, regarding the universe with an agreeable smile. He began to remember. He could not remember very well, because of a steam roundabout that was beginning in his head. And he knew he had been disagreeable at home, just because they wanted to be happy. They were quite right; life should be as gay as possible. He would go home and make it up, and reassure them. And why not take some of this delightful toadstool with him, for them to eat? A hatful, no less. Some of those red ones with white spots as well, and a few yellow. He had been a dull dog, an enemy to merriment; he would make up for it. It would be gay to turn his coat-sleeves inside out, and stick some yellow gorse into his waistcoat pockets. Then home – singing – for a jolly evening.

After the departure of Mr Coombes, Jennie discontinued playing, and turned round on the music-stool again. 'What a fuss about nothing!' said Jennie.

'You see, Mr Clarence, what I've got to put up with,' said Mrs Coombes.

'He is a bit hasty,' said Mr Clarence judicially.

'He ain't got the slightest sense of our position,' said Mrs Coombes; 'that's what I complain of. He cares for nothing but his old shop; and if I have a bit of company, or buy anything to keep myself decent, or get any little thing I want out of the housekeeping money, there's disagreeables. "Economy," he says; "struggle for life", and all that. He lies awake of nights about it, worrying how he can screw me out of a shilling. He wanted us to eat Dorset butter once. If once I was to give in to him – there!'

'Of course,' said Jennie.

'If a man values a woman,' said Mr Clarence, lounging back in the arm-chair, 'he must be prepared to make sacrifices for her. For my own part,' said Mr Clarence, with his eye on Jennie, 'I shouldn't think of marrying till I was in a position to do the thing in style. It's downright selfishness. A man ought to go through the rough-and-tumble by himself, and not drag her—'

'I don't agree altogether with that,' said Jennie. 'I don't see why a man shouldn't have a woman's help, provided he doesn't treat her meanly, you know. It's meanness—'

'You wouldn't believe,' said Mrs Coombes. 'But I was a fool to 'ave 'im. I might 'ave known. If it 'adn't been for my father, we shouldn't 'ave 'ad not a carriage to our wedding.'

'Lord! he didn't stick out at that?' said Mr Clarence, quite shocked.

'Said he wanted the money for his stock, or some such rubbish. Why, he wouldn't have a woman in to help me once a week if it wasn't for my standing out plucky. And the fusses he makes about money – comes to me, well, pretty near crying, with sheets of paper and figgers. "If only we can tide over this year," he says, "the business is bound to go." "If only we can tide over this year," I says; "then it'll be, if only we can tide over next year. I know you," I says. "And you don't catch me screwing myself lean and ugly. Why didn't you marry a slavey?" I says, "if you wanted one – instead of a respectable girl," I says.'

So Mrs Coombes. But we will not follow this unedifying conversation further. Suffice it that Mr Coombes was very satisfactorily disposed of, and they had a snug little time round the fire. Then Mrs Coombes went to get the tea, and Jennie sat coquettishly on the arm of Mr Clarence's chair until the tea-things clattered outside. 'What was that I heard?' asked Mrs Coombes playfully, as she entered, and there was badinage about kissing. They were just sitting down to the little circular table when the first intimation of Mr Coombes' return was heard.

This was a fumbling at the latch of the front door.

''Ere's my lord,' said Mrs Coombes. 'Went out like a lion and comes back like a lamb, I'll lay.'

Something fell over in the shop: a chair, it sounded like. Then there was a sound as of some complicated step exercise in the passage. Then the door opened and Coombes appeared. But it was Coombes transfigured. The immaculate collar had been torn carelessly from his throat. His carefully-brushed silk hat, half-full of a crush of fungi, was under one arm; his coat was inside out, and his waistcoat adorned with bunches of yellow-blossomed furze. These little eccentricities of Sunday costume, however, were quite overshadowed by the change in his face; it was livid white, his eyes were unnaturally large and bright, and his pale blue lips were drawn back in a cheerless grin. 'Merry!' he said. He had stopped dancing to open the door. 'Rational 'njoyment. Dance.' He made three fantastic steps into the room, and stood bowing.

'Jim!' shrieked Mrs Coombes, and Mr Clarence sat petrified, with a dropping lower jaw.

'Tea,' said Mr Coombes. 'Jol' thing, tea. Tose-stools, too. Brosher.'

'He's drunk,' said Jennie in a weak voice. Never before had she seen this intense pallor in a drunken man, or such shining, dilated eyes.

Mr Coombes held out a handful of scarlet agaric to Mr Clarence. 'Jo' stuff,' said he; 'ta' some.'

At that moment he was genial. Then at the sight of their startled faces he changed, with the swift transition of insanity, into overbearing fury. And it seemed as if he had suddenly recalled the quarrel of his departure. In such a huge voice as Mrs Coombes had never heard before, he shouted, 'My house. I'm master 'ere. Eat what I give yer!' He bawled this, as it seemed, without an effort, without a violent gesture, standing there as motionless as one who whispers, holding out a handful of fungus.

Clarence approved himself a coward. He could not meet the mad fury in Coombes' eyes; he rose to his feet, pushing back his chair, and turned, stooping. At that Coombes rushed at him. Jennie saw her opportunity, and, with the ghost of a shriek, made for the door. Mrs Coombes followed her. Clarence tried to dodge. Over went the tea-table with a smash as Coombes clutched him by the collar and tried to thrust the fungus into his mouth. Clarence was content to leave his collar behind him, and shot out into the passage with red patches of fly agaric still adherent to his face. 'Shut 'im in!' cried Mrs Coombes, and would have closed the door, but her supports deserted her; Jennie saw the shop door open, and vanished thereby, locking it behind her, while Clarence went on hastily into the kitchen. Mr Coombes came heavily against the door, and Mrs Coombes, finding the key was inside, fled upstairs and locked herself in the spare bedroom.

So the new convert to *joie de vivre* emerged upon the passage, his decorations a little scattered, but that respectable hatful of fungi still under his arm. He hesitated at the three ways, and decided on the kitchen. Whereupon Clarence, who was fumbling with the key, gave up the attempt to imprison his host, and fled into the scullery, only to be captured before he could open the door into the yard. Mr Clarence is singularly reticent of the details of what occurred. It seems that Mr Coombes' transitory irritation had vanished again, and he was once more a genial playfellow. And as there were knives and meat choppers about, Clarence very generously resolved to humour him and so avoid anything tragic. It is beyond dispute that Mr Coombes played with Mr Clarence to his heart's content; they could not have been more playful and familiar if they had known each other for years. He insisted gaily on Clarence trying the fungi, and, after a friendly tussle, was smitten with remorse at the mess he was making of his guest's face. It also appears that Clarence was dragged under the sink and his face scrubbed with the blacking brush – he being still resolved to humour the lunatic at any cost – and that finally, in a somewhat dishevelled, chipped, and discoloured condition, he was assisted to his coat and shown out by the back door, the shopway being barred by Jennie. Mr Coombes' wandering thoughts then turned to Jennie. Jennie had been unable to unfasten the shop door, but she shot the bolts against Mr Coombes' latch-key, and remained in possession of the shop for the rest of the evening.

It would appear that Mr Coombes then returned to the kitchen, still in pursuit of gaiety, and, albeit a strict Good Templar, drank (or spilt down the front of the first and only frock-coat) no less than five bottles of the stout Mrs Coombes insisted upon having for her health's sake. He made cheerful noises by breaking off the necks of the bottles with several of his wife's wedding-present dinner-plates, and during the earlier part of this great drunk he sang divers merry ballads. He cut his finger rather badly with one of the bottles – the only blood-shed in this story – and what with that, and the systematic convulsion of his inexperienced physiology by the liquorish brand of Mrs Coombes' stout, it may be the evil of the fungus poison was somehow allayed. But we prefer to draw a veil over the concluding incidents of this Sunday afternoon. They ended in the coal cellar, in a deep and healing sleep.

✌ ✌ ✌

An interval of five years elapsed. Again it was a Sunday afternoon in October, and again Mr Coombes walked through the pine wood beyond the canal. He was still the same dark-eyed, black-moustached little man that he was at the outset of the story, but his double chin was now scarcely so illusory as it had been. His overcoat was new, with a velvet lapel, and a stylish collar with turn-down corners, free of any coarse starchiness, had replaced the original all-round article. His hat was glossy, his gloves newish – though one finger had split and been carefully mended. And a casual observer would have noticed about him a certain rectitude of bearing, a certain erectness of head that marks the man who thinks well of himself. He was a master now, with three assistants. Beside him walked a larger sunburnt parody of himself, his brother Tom, just back from Australia. They were recapitulating their early struggles, and Mr Coombes had just been making a financial statement.

'It's a very nice little business, Jim,' said brother Tom. 'In these days of competition you're jolly lucky to have worked it up so. And you're jolly lucky, too, to have a wife who's willing to help like yours does.'

'Between ourselves,' said Mr Coombes, 'it wasn't always so. It wasn't always like this. To begin with, the missus was a bit giddy. Girls are funny creatures.'

'Dear me!'

'Yes. You'd hardly think it, but she was downright extravagant, and always having slaps at me. I was a bit too easy and loving, and all that, and she thought the whole blessed show was run for her. Turned the 'ouse into a regular caravansery, always having her relations and girls from business in, and their chaps. Comic songs a' Sunday, it was getting to, and driving trade away. And she was making eyes at the chaps, too! I tell you, Tom, the place wasn't my own.'

'Shouldn't 'a' thought it.'

'It was so. Well – I reasoned with her. I said, "I ain't a duke, to keep a wife like a pet animal. I married you for 'elp and company." I said, "You got to 'elp and pull the business through." She wouldn't 'ear of it. "Very well," I says; "I'm a mild man till I'm roused," I says, "and it's getting to that." But she wouldn't 'ear of no warnings.'

'Well?'

'It's the way with women. She didn't think I 'ad it in me to be roused. Women of her sort (between ourselves, Tom) don't respect a man until they're a bit afraid of him. So I just broke out to show her. In comes a girl named Jennie, that used to work with her, and her chap. We 'ad a bit of a row, and I came out 'ere – it was just such another day as this – and I thought it all out. Then I went back and pitched into them.'

'You did?'

'I did. I was mad, I can tell you, I wasn't going to 'it 'er, if I could 'elp it, so I went back and licked into this chap, just to show 'er what I could do. 'E was a big chap, too. Well, I chucked him, and smashed things about, and gave 'er a scaring, and she ran up and locked 'erself into the spare room.'

'Well?'

'That's all. I says to 'er the next morning. "Now you know," I says, "what I'm like when I'm roused." And I didn't have to say anything more.'

'And you've been happy ever after, eh?'

'So to speak. There's nothing like putting your foot down with them. If it 'adn't been for that afternoon I should 'a' been tramping the roads now, and she'd 'a' been grumbling at me, and all her family grumbling for bringing her to poverty – I know their little ways. But we're all right now. And it's a very decent little business, as you say.'

They proceeded on their way meditatively. 'Women are funny creatures,' said Brother Tom.

'They want a firm hand,' says Coombes.

'What a lot of these funguses there are about here!' remarked Brother Tom presently. 'I can't see what use they are in the world.'

Mr Coombes looked. 'I dessay they're sent for some wise purpose,' said Mr Coombes.

And that was as much thanks as the purple pileus ever got for maddening this absurd little man to the pitch of decisive action, and so altering the whole course of his life.

Comparing the texts

Now that you have read both stories, think about the following points of contrast and comparison.

- Which of the two central characters is more appealing to you? How has the author achieved this?
- How does the **structure** of each story differ, and does this affect your enjoyment of them?
- What features of short stories as a genre (form of writing) can you identify from these texts?
- Does one story use **language** in a more effective way than the other?
- How do the different **cultural** and historical **settings** of the stories influence the authors' ideas and attitudes and the way you respond to them?
- Is it significant that one story is about a female character and is written by a female author whereas the central character in the other story, written by a man, is male?

Writing about the texts

When you have thought about these issues and have discussed any other points raised by your teacher, think about planning a written response to the stories using one of the following tasks.

Your teacher may give you additional notes to help you identify significant details and references, but remember that the freshness and originality of your own response is important. If you find these stories difficult to read and understand, it may be better first to consider tasks in later chapters of this book. When you have read other texts, you may prefer to link one or more of them with the Shields or Wells stories, using an idea from Chapter 6, or an original task which you have thought about yourself, following a discussion with your teacher.

Tasks

1 In both *Mrs. Turner Cutting the Grass* and *The Purple Pileus*, the central character is seen in some ways as pitiable by other characters in the story. Readers of both stories can appreciate some of the main characters' strengths. What do you feel about Mrs Turner and Mr Coombes, and what similarities and differences are there in the **techniques** used by the authors to influence your reactions?

2 *Mrs. Turner Cutting the Grass* and *The Purple Pileus* are both comic stories, but both have serious things to say about the **values** and opinions of the societies and times in which they are set. Compare the ways in which Carol Shields and H.G. Wells use comedy to make important points. Who is the more successful in your view, and why?

3 In both *Mrs. Turner Cutting the Grass* and *The Purple Pileus*, the author occasionally addresses you, the reader, directly. In what ways does this technique add to, or spoil, the author's success in getting across a message?

Glossaries

Carol Shields, *Mrs. Turner Cutting the Grass*

affronted	offended
antebellum	dating from before the Civil War
aura	invisible power
avuncular	friendly
banality	commonness, lack of taste
baseboards	skirting-boards
buoyant	cheerful
capillary	thin-walled blood vessel
caragana	shrub used for hedging
catcher	grass-box for a lawn mower
catharsis	purification or release of feelings or emotions
cellulite	layers of fat just below the skin
chapbooks	slim volumes
cologne	perfume

commonality	belonging together
conspiratorial	secret
counterpoint	set in contrast against something else
crepe-soled	soles of shoes made from a crinkly-surfaced rubber compound
defilement	pollution
ecosystem	the relationship between a community and its environment
foundling	abandoned child
furies	snake-haired goddesses in classical mythology
fused	joined
garish	colourful in an overbright, crude way
gnarled	twisted
halter (top)	fastened behind neck and waist, leaving the back and arms bare
hollers	shouts
incised	carved
ironic	unexpected in a strange or amusing way
irony	humorous, unexpected inconsistency
irreconcilable	unable to be brought together
lapped	folded
morose	gloomy
paltry	small, insignificant
phonograph	early type of gramophone or record-player
providential	fortunate
pug	small and plump (like the breed of dog)
rabid	suffering from rabies
relish	enjoy
resonant	deep, intense
rouge	cosmetic used to add colour to cheeks
saccharine	sweetener used instead of sugar by slimmers
striated	grooved, wavy
tacky	in bad taste
transcendence	excellence
unperceived	unnoticed
wicker	made of flexible twigs of wood

H.G. Wells, *The Purple Pileus*

acrid	unpleasantly sharp (smell)
adherent	sticking
approved	considered
astrachan	fur made from lambswool
badinage	teasing
bearing	behaviour, attitude
blacking brush	brush used to apply black polish to ranges or fireplaces
blasphemies	disrespectful language, mild swearing
blight	damage
capital	money
caravansery	spectacle, show
convulsion	upheaval

coquettishly	flirtatiously
courting	(lovers) going out together
cravat	scarf worn instead of tie
culminations	climaxes
determine	make out, decide
dilated	enlarged
dishevelled	untidy
disrepute	lack of respectability
divers	various
drab	cheap material
elapsed	passed
emitting	giving off
exasperated	annoyed
flounces	ornamental edgings sewn onto dresses
forthwith	immediately
frock-coat	long man's jacket with tails
gaiety	happiness
genial	happy, friendly
giddy	foolish
Good Templar	someone who does not drink alcohol
illusory	apparent, not real
immaculate	neat, tidy
incensed	extremely angry
inexorably	relentlessly, immovably
intended	fiance
intimated	suggested
intimation	suggestion, sign
joie de vivre	happiness
judicially	carefully
juice	phonetic spelling of 'deuce' (devil)
laborious	hard
lank	tall and thin
lay	bet
licked	thrashed
liquorish	laxative
livid	greyish
loquacious	talkative
meagre	limited
meditatively	thoughtfully
melancholia	misery, unhappiness
melancholy	miserable
Mephistopheles	the devil
mill-race	fast-flowing stream supplying a water-wheel at a mill
nourished	fed
pallor	paleness
parody	copy
penurious	mean
perceived	saw, understood

petrified	terrified
piously	religiously
plucky	bravely
pungent	strong, unpleasant
rash	hasty, unwise
rational	reasonable
recapitulated	repeated, went over in his mind
rectitude	correctness
resolve	decision
resolved	decided
respiration	breathing
restraints	limits
reticent	unwilling to talk about
rigour	harshness
shindy	noise
slaps	criticisms
smitten	overcome
stout	type of beer
strident	piercing, loud, unpleasant
suffice it	it is enough to say that
sufficiency	having just enough to live on
systematic	orderly
transfigured	changed dramatically
transition	change
transitory	short-lived
unedifying	unimproving, unpleasant
wrathful	angry

Guilty consciences: genres from different periods

Introduction

This chapter gives you the opportunity to compare different genres. A genre is a type or form of writing which has particular qualities or characteristics, such as the short story (which was the genre of both texts used in Chapter 1). The following four texts comprise a **ballad**, a short story, a complete short **fiction** text in the form of a supposed **autobiographical** confession, and a television **monologue**. They are linked by the theme of guilt or suspicion and cover more than 150 years of writing, from the Dickens written in the first half of the nineteenth century to the Bennett television script written at the end of the twentieth century.

Comparing genres such as **prose** fiction, **poetry** and **drama** can be a useful way of understanding how writers use different techniques and styles of language, appropriate to the form they have chosen, to convey their ideas and feelings. Generally speaking, a ballad would be written for live, dramatic reading to a fairly small group of people; short stories are often read silently and in private; while a television play is seen by a potentially huge number of viewers, but may be performed and recorded in an almost empty studio. These various circumstances place different demands and pressures on writers and performers, and are likely to have different effects on you, the reader, listener or viewer.

- Ballads tell a simple story, usually in a straightforward **chronological** sequence, using repetitive **rhythms** and rhyme schemes to make them easy to memorise and to produce an almost hypnotic effect on listeners, who are thus drawn into the poem and its subject-matter.

- Prose fiction, whether it is a full-length novel or a short story, can make use of opportunities for description and reflection (by the characters or by the author). It also allows the use of particular techniques or **devices** such as **flashback**s or **multiple viewpoint**s, where more than one character gives an account of, or a reaction to, an event or situation. If the reader finds it difficult to follow, or wants to check on something, it is easy to re-read a passage or linger over the meaning of a word or phrase. You can't do that if you're listening to a ballad in performance – once spoken, it's over!

- A television script presents its own challenges and possibilities. You can revisit it if you don't understand something – by using a video recorder or waiting for a repeat showing, for example – but this is not as direct or perhaps as convenient as lingering over a piece of printed text. You can, of course, study the published script (as you will be doing here), but unless the writer uses a vast amount of detailed direction to the actor (which is not the case in the text included here) you, the reader, have to do a great deal of work in interpreting the meaning of the words on the page. Unless the writer uses a device such as **voiceover**, which can appear very clumsy unless skilfully done, there are not the same opportunities for the author to describe or reflect as in prose texts. However, the use of actors to deliver the script means that facial expression, **body language** and actions can be used to convey meaning in effective ways which printed text on the page cannot do.

These basic genre differences have huge implications for choices in the use of language and structure made by writers, for the attitudes they adopt towards their readers, listeners or viewers, and for the impact or effect the text has on its **audience**.

They also have implications for how you write about the texts, because you need to measure the success of each piece of writing against the genre chosen by the author. It would be silly, for example, to criticise the **repetition** of words or whole lines in Hardy's ballad, because that is a feature of the ballad form; instead, you should ask yourself why the author has chosen to work within this convention or tradition. It would be equally pointless to complain at the lack of description in Bennett's television script. You certainly should consider how successfully genre features such as these are used, but you must judge how relevant they are to what each writer is trying to achieve within the form he or she has chosen to use.

Reading the Thomas Hardy

The first text is *A Trampwoman's Tragedy*, written by Thomas Hardy in 1902. The subtitle (182–) shows that it is set some eighty years earlier, and Hardy is deliberately writing in an old-fashioned form, using a style which includes **archaic** and **dialect** words. Like much of Hardy's writing, the poem is set in the fictional area of Wessex, which covers the modern counties of south-western and central southern England, in this case, Somerset. The explanatory notes at the end were written by the author himself.

As a ballad, the poem is best appreciated if you read it aloud. While you listen to it, think about:

- the effects achieved by the repetition of phrases, words and sounds
- the effects of Hardy's choice of language, for example, the use of archaic, dialect and **'poetic'** words
- why Hardy uses so many place-names and adds the detailed notes at the end of the poem – how does this add to your understanding and enjoyment of the poem?
- whether, and how, the writer tries to get you to sympathise with the trampwoman
- the main idea that Hardy intends to convey through the events described in this poem.

A Trampwoman's Tragedy (182–)

I

From Wynyard's Gap the livelong day,
    The livelong day,
We beat afoot the northward way
    We had travelled times before.
The sun-blaze burning on our backs,
Our shoulders sticking to our packs,
By fosseway, fields, and turnpike tracks
    We skirted sad Sedge-Moor.

II

Full twenty miles we jaunted on,
    We jaunted on,—
My fancy-man, and jeering John,
    And Mother Lee, and I.
And, as the sun drew down to west,
We climbed the toilsome Poldon crest,
And saw, of landskip sights the best,
    The inn that beamed thereby.

III

For months we had padded side by side,
    Ay, side by side
Through the Great Forest, Blackmoor wide,
    And where the Parret ran.
We'd faced the gusts on Mendip ridge,
Had crossed the Yeo unhelped by bridge,
Been stung by every Marshwood midge,
    I and my fancy-man.

IV

Lone inns we loved, my man and I,
    My man and I;
"King's Stag," "Windwhistle" high and dry,
    "The Horse" on Hintock Green.
The cosy house at Wynyard's Gap,
"The Hut" renowned on Bredy Knap,
And many another wayside tap
    Where folk might sit unseen.

V

Now as we trudged—O deadly day,
    O deadly day!—
I teased my fancy man in play
    And wanton idleness.
I walked alongside jeering John,
I laid his hand my waist upon;
I would not bend my glances on
    My lover's dark distress.

VI

Thus Poldon top at last we won,
    At last we won,
And gained the inn at sink of sun
    Far-famed as "Marshal's Elm."
Beneath us figured tor and lea,
From Mendip to the western sea—
I doubt if finer sight there be
    Within this royal realm.

VII

Inside the settle all a-row—
    All four a-row
We sat, I next to John, to show
    That he had wooed and won.
And then he took me on his knee,
And swore it was his turn to be
My favoured mate, and Mother Lee
    Passed to my former one.

VIII

Then in a voice I had never heard,
    I had never heard,
My only Love to me: "One word,
    My lady, if you please!
Whose is the child you are like to bear?—
His? After all my months o' care?"
God knows 'twas not! But, O despair!
    I nodded—still to tease.

IX

Then up he sprung, and with his knife—
    And with his knife
He let out jeering Johnny's life,
    Yes; there, at set of sun.
The slant ray through the window nigh
Gilded John's blood and glazing eye,
Ere scarcely Mother Lee and I
    Knew that the deed was done.

X

The taverns tell the gloomy tale,
    The gloomy tale,
How that at Ivel-chester jail
    My Love, my sweetheart swung;
Though stained till now by no misdeed
Save one horse ta'en in time o' need;
(Blue Jimmy stole right many a steed
    Ere his last fling he flung.)

XI

Thereaft I walked the world alone,
    Alone, alone!
On his death-day I gave my groan
    And dropt his dead-born child.
'Twas nigh the jail, beneath a tree,
None tending me; for Mother Lee
Had died at Glaston, leaving me
    Unfriended on the wild.

XII

And in the night as I lay weak,
    As I lay weak,
The leaves a-falling on my cheek,
    The red moon low declined—
The ghost of him I'd die to kiss
Rose up and said: "Ah, tell me this!
Was the child mine, or was it his?
    Speak, that I rest may find!"

XIII

O doubt not but I told him then,
    I told him then,
That I had kept me from all men
    Since we joined lips and swore.
Whereat he smiled, and thinned away
As the wind stirred to call up day . . .
—'Tis past! And here alone I stray
    Haunting the Western Moor.

Thomas Hardy

Notes.—"Windwhistle" (Stanza IV.). The highness and dryness of Windwhistle Inn was impressed upon the writer two or three years ago, when, after climbing on a hot afternoon to the beautiful spot near which it stands and entering the inn for tea, he was informed by the landlady that none could be had, unless he would fetch water from a valley half a mile off, the house containing not a drop, owing to its situation. However, a tantalizing row of full barrels behind her back testified to a wetness of a certain sort, which was not at that time desired.

"Marshal's Elm" (Stanza VI.), so picturesquely situated, is no longer an inn, though the house, or part of it, still remains. It used to exhibit a fine old swinging sign.

"Blue Jimmy" (Stanza X.) was a notorious horse-stealer of Wessex in those days, who appropriated more than a hundred horses before he was caught, among others one belonging to a neighbour of the writer's grandfather. He was hanged at the now demolished Ivel-chester or Ilchester jail above mentioned—that building formerly of so many sinister associations in the minds of the local peasantry, and the continual haunt of fever, which at last led to its condemnation. Its site is now an innocent-looking green meadow.

April 1902.

Reading the Wilkie Collins

Wilkie Collins' story *Mr Policeman and the Cook* was published in 1887, just two years before his death. Earlier in his life, he had been one of the first writers of crime and detective stories with his two most famous novels, *The Woman in White* and *The Moonstone*. This short story shows his continuing fascination with why people commit (and cover up) crimes, but it also shows his liking for a lively story with plenty of action, sometimes making use of rather far-fetched **coincidences** or chance events in the **plot**.

When reading this text, think about:

- whether Collins makes the **narrator** appear sympathetic to us, and how he does this
- how different characters in the story are brought to life by the author's descriptions of them, by their actions and through their speech
- how humour is used, and to what effect
- whether the part played by coincidence or chance spoils your enjoyment of the story
- comparisons and contrasts between this story and the Hardy poem in theme, tone and overall effect.

by Wilkie Collins

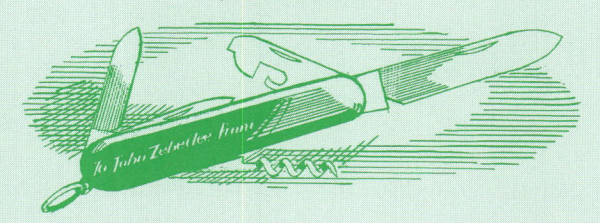

Mr Policeman and the Cook
A First Word for Myself

BEFORE THE DOCTOR left me one evening, I asked him how much longer I was likely to live. He answered: 'It's not easy to say; you may die before I can get back to you in the morning, or you may live to the end of the month.'

I was alive enough on the next morning to think of the needs of my soul, and (being a member of the Roman Catholic Church) to send for the priest.

The history of my sins, related in confession, included blameworthy neglect of a duty which I owed to the laws of my country. In the priest's opinion – and I agreed with him – I was bound to make public acknowledgment of my fault, as an act of penance becoming to a Catholic Englishman. We concluded, thereupon, to try a division of labour. I related the circumstances, while his reverence took the pen, and put the matter into shape.

Here follows what came of it: –

I

When I was a young man of five and twenty, I became a member of the London police-force. After nearly two years' ordinary experience of the responsible and ill-paid duties of that vocation, I found myself employed on my first serious and terrible case of official inquiry – relating to nothing less than the crime of Murder.

The circumstances were these: –

I was then attached to a station in the northern district of London – which I beg permission not to mention more particularly. On a certain Monday in the week, I took my turn of night duty. Up to four in the morning, nothing occurred at the station-house out of the ordinary way. It was then spring time, and, between the gas and the fire, the room became rather hot. I went to the door to get a breath of fresh air – much to the surprise of our Inspector on duty, who was constitutionally a chilly man. There was a fine rain falling; and a nasty damp in the air sent me back to the fireside. I don't suppose I had sat down for more than a minute when the swinging-door was violently pushed open. A frantic woman ran in with a scream, and said: 'Is this the station-house?'

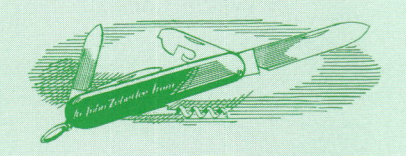

Our Inspector (otherwise an excellent officer) had, by some perversity of nature, a hot temper in his chilly constitution. 'Why, bless the woman, can't you see it is?' he says. 'What's the matter now?'

'Murder's the matter!' she burst out. 'For God's sake come back with me. It's at Mrs Crosscapel's lodging-house, number 14, Lehigh Street. A young woman has murdered her husband in the night! With a knife, sir. She says she thinks she did it in her sleep.'

I confess I was startled by this; and the third man on duty (a sergeant) seemed to feel it too. She was a nice-looking young woman, even in her terrified condition, just out of bed, with her clothes huddled on anyhow. I was partial in those days to a tall figure – and she was, as they say, my style. I put a chair for her; and the sergeant poked the fire. As for the Inspector, nothing ever upset *him*. He questioned her as coolly as if it had been a case of petty larceny.

'Have you seen the murdered man?' he asked.

'No, sir.'

'Or the wife?'

'No, sir. I didn't dare go into the room; I only heard about it!'

'Oh? And who are You? One of the lodgers?'

'No, sir. I'm the cook.'

'Isn't there a master in the house?'

'Yes, sir. He's frightened out of his wits. And the housemaid's gone for the Doctor. It all falls on the poor servants, of course. Oh, why did I ever set foot in that horrible house?'

The poor soul burst out crying, and shivered from head to foot. The Inspector made a note of her statement, and then asked her to read it, and sign it with her name. The object of this proceeding was to get her to come near enough to give him the opportunity of smelling her breath. 'When people make extraordinary statements,' he afterwards said to me, 'it sometimes saves trouble to satisfy yourself that they are not drunk. I've known them to be mad – but not often. You will generally find *that* in their eyes.'

She roused herself, and signed her name – 'Priscilla Thurlby'. The Inspector's own test proved her to be sober; and her eyes – of a nice light blue colour, mild and pleasant, no doubt, when they were not staring with fear, and red with crying – satisfied him (as I supposed) that she was not mad. He turned the case over to me, in the first instance. I saw that he didn't believe in it, even yet.

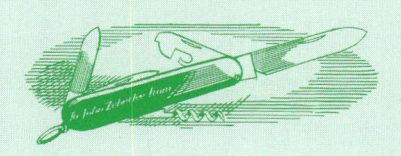

'Go back with her to the house,' he says. 'This may be a stupid hoax, or a quarrel exaggerated. See to it yourself, and hear what the Doctor says. If it *is* serious, send word back here directly, and let nobody enter the place or leave it till we come. Stop! You know the form if any statement is volunteered?'

'Yes, sir. I am to caution the persons that whatever they say will be taken down, and may be used against them.'

'Quite right. You'll be an Inspector yourself one of these days. Now, Miss!' With that he dismissed her, under my care.

Lehigh Street was not very far off – about twenty minutes' walk from the station. I confess I thought the Inspector had been rather hard on Priscilla. She was herself naturally angry with him. 'What does he mean,' she says, 'by talking of a hoax? I wish he was as frightened as I am. This is the first time I have been out at service, sir – and I did think I had found a respectable place.'

I said very little to her – feeling, if the truth must be told, rather anxious about the duty committed to me. On reaching the house the door was opened from within, before I could knock. A gentleman stepped out, who proved to be the Doctor. He stopped the moment he saw me.

'You must be careful, policeman,' he says. 'I found the man lying on his back, in bed, dead – with the knife that had killed him left sticking in the wound.'

Hearing this, I felt the necessity of sending at once to the station. Where could I find a trustworthy messenger? I took the liberty of asking the Doctor if he would repeat to the police what he had already said to me. The station was not much out of his way home. He kindly granted my request.

The landlady (Mrs Crosscapel) joined us while we were talking. She was still a young woman; not easily frightened, as far as I could see, even by a murder in the house. Her husband was in the passage behind her. He looked old enough to be her father; and he so trembled with terror that some people might have taken him for the guilty person. I removed the key from the street door, after locking it; and I said to the landlady: 'Nobody must leave the house, or enter the house, till the Inspector comes. I must examine the premises to see if anyone has broken in.'

'There is the key of the area gate,' she said, in answer to me. 'It's always kept locked. Come downstairs, and see for yourself.' Priscilla went with us. Her mistress set her to work to light the kitchen fire. 'Some of us,' says Mrs Crosscapel, 'may be the better for a cup of tea.' I remarked that she took things easy, under the circumstances. She answered that the landlady of a London lodging-house could not afford to lose her wits, no matter what might happen.

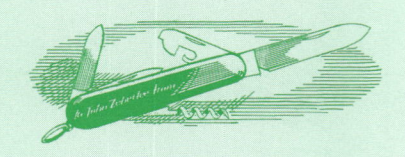

I found the gate locked, and the shutters of the kitchen window fastened. The back kitchen and back door were secured in the same way. No person was concealed anywhere. Returning upstairs, I examined the front parlour window. There again, the barred shutters answered for the security of that room. A cracked voice spoke through the door of the back parlour. 'The policeman can come in,' it said, 'if he will promise not to look at me.' I turned to the landlady for information. 'It's my parlour lodger, Miss Mybus,' she said, 'a most respectable lady.' Going into the room, I saw something rolled up perpendicularly in the bed curtains. Miss Mybus had made herself modestly invisible in that way. Having now satisfied my mind about the security of the lower part of the house, and having the keys safe in my pocket, I was ready to go upstairs.

On our way to the upper regions I asked if there had been any visitors on the previous day. There had been only two visitors, friends of the lodgers – and Mrs Crosscapel herself had let them both out. My next enquiry related to the lodgers themselves. On the ground floor there was Miss Mybus. On the first floor (occupying both rooms) Mr Barfield, an old bachelor, employed in a merchant's office. On the second floor, in the front room, Mr John Zebedee, the murdered man, and his wife. In the back room, Mr Deluc; described as a cigar agent, and supposed to be a Creole gentleman from Martinique. In the front garret, Mr and Mrs Crosscapel. In the back garret, the cook and the housemaid. These were the inhabitants, regularly accounted for. I asked about the servants. 'Both excellent characters,' says the landlady, 'or they would not be in my service.'

We reached the second floor, and found the housemaid on the watch outside the door of the front room. Not as nice a woman, personally, as the cook, and sadly frightened of course. Her mistress had posted her, to give the alarm in the case of an outbreak on the part of Mrs Zebedee, kept locked up in the room. My arrival relieved the housemaid of further responsibility. She ran downstairs to her fellow servant in the kitchen.

I asked Mrs Crosscapel how and when the alarm of the murder had been given.

'Soon after three this morning,' says she, 'I was woke by the screams of Mrs Zebedee. I found her out here on the landing, and Mr Deluc, in great alarm, trying to quiet her. Sleeping in the next room, he had only to open his door, when her screams woke him. "My dear John's murdered! I am the miserable wretch – I did it in my sleep!" She repeated those frantic words over and over again, until she dropped in a swoon. Mr Deluc and I carried her back into the bedroom. We both thought the poor creature had been driven distracted by some dreadful dream. But when we got to the bedside – don't ask me what we saw; the Doctor has told you about it already. I was once a nurse in a hospital, and accustomed, as such, to horrid sights. It turned me cold and giddy, notwithstanding. As for Mr Deluc, I thought *he* would have had a fainting fit next.'

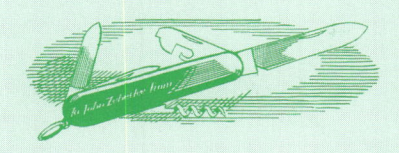

Hearing this, I enquired if Mrs Zebedee had said or done any strange things since she had been Mrs Crosscapel's lodger.

'You think she's mad?' says the landlady. 'And anybody would be of your mind, when a woman accuses herself of murdering her husband in her sleep. All I can say is that, up to this morning, a more quiet, sensible, well-behaved little person than Mrs Zebedee I never met with. Only just married, mind, and as fond of her unfortunate husband as a woman could be. I should have called them a pattern couple, in their own line of life.'

There was no more to be said on the landing. We unlocked the door and went into the room.

2

He lay in bed on his back as the Doctor had described him. On the left side of his nightgown, just over his heart, the blood on the linen told its terrible tale. As well as one could judge, looking unwillingly at a dead face, he must have been a handsome young man in his lifetime. It was a sight to sadden anybody – but I think the most painful sensation was when my eyes fell next on his miserable wife.

She was down on the floor, crouched up in a corner – a dark little woman, smartly dressed in gay colours. Her black hair and her big brown eyes made the horrid paleness of her face look even more deadly white than perhaps it really was. She stared straight at us without appearing to see us. We spoke to her, and she never answered a word. She might have been dead – like her husband – except that she perpetually picked at her fingers, and shuddered every now and then as if she was cold. I went to her and tried to lift her up. She shrank back with a cry that well-nigh frightened me – not because it was loud, but because it was more like the cry of some animal than of a human being. However quietly she might have behaved in the landlady's previous experience of her, she was beside herself now. I might have been moved by a natural pity for her, or I might have been completely upset in my mind – I only know this, I could not persuade myself that she was guilty. I even said to Mrs Crosscapel, 'I don't believe she did it.'

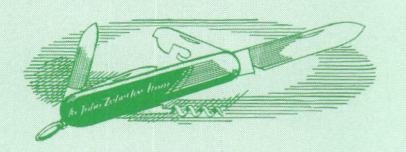

While I spoke, there was a knock at the door. I went downstairs at once, and admitted (to my great relief) the Inspector, accompanied by one of our men.

He waited downstairs to hear my report, and he approved of what I had done. 'It looks as if the murder had been committed by somebody in the house.' Saying this, he left the man below, and went up with me to the second floor.

Before he had been a minute in the room, he discovered an object which had escaped my observation.

It was the knife that had done the deed.

The Doctor had found it left in the body – had withdrawn it to probe the wound – and had laid it on the bedside table. It was one of those useful knives which contain a saw, a corkscrew, and other like implements. The big blade fastened back, when open, with a spring. Except where the blood was on it, it was as bright as when it had been purchased. A small metal plate was fastened to the horn handle, containing an inscription, only partly engraved, which ran thus: '*To John Zebedee, from* —' There it stopped, strangely enough.

Who or what had interrupted the engraver's work? It was impossible even to guess. Nevertheless, the Inspector was encouraged.

'This ought to help us,' he said – and then he gave an attentive ear (looking all the while at the poor creature in the corner) to what Mrs Crosscapel had to tell him.

The landlady having done, he said he must now see the lodger who slept in the next bedchamber.

Mr Deluc made his appearance, standing at the door of the room, and turning away his head with horror from the sight inside.

He was wrapped in a splendid blue dressing-gown, with a golden girdle and trimmings. His scanty brownish hair curled (whether artificially or not, I am unable to say) in little ringlets. His complexion was yellow; his greenish-brown eyes were of the sort called 'goggle' – they looked as if they might drop out of his face, if you held a spoon under them. His moustache and goat's beard were beautifully oiled; and, to complete his equipment, he had a long black cigar in his mouth.

'It isn't insensibility to this terrible tragedy,' he explained. 'My nerves have been shattered, Mr Policeman, and I can only repair the mischief in this way. Be pleased to excuse and feel for me.'

The Inspector questioned this witness sharply and closely. He was not a man to be misled by appearances: but I could see that he was far from liking, or even trusting, Mr Deluc. Nothing came of the examination, except what Mrs Crosscapel had in substance already mentioned to me. Mr Deluc returned to his room.

'How long has he been lodging with you?' the Inspector asked, as soon as his back was turned.

'Nearly a year,' the landlady answered.

'Did he give you a reference?'

'As good a reference as I could wish for.' Thereupon, she mentioned the names of a well-known firm of cigar merchants in the City. The Inspector noted the information in his pocket-book.

I would rather not relate in detail what happened next: it is too distressing to be dwelt on. Let me only say that the poor demented woman was taken away in a cab to the station-house. The Inspector possessed himself of the knife, and of a book found on the floor, called *The World of Sleep*. The portmanteau containing the luggage was locked – and then the door of the room was secured, the keys in both cases being left in my charge. My instructions were to remain in the house, and allow nobody to leave it, until I heard again shortly from the Inspector.

3

The coroner's inquest was adjourned; and the examination before the magistrate ended in a remand – Mrs Zebedee being in no condition to understand the proceedings in either case. The surgeon reported her to be completely prostrated by a terrible nervous shock. When he was asked if he considered her to have been a sane woman before the murder took place, he refused to answer positively at that time.

A week passed. The murdered man was buried; his old father attending the funeral. I occasionally saw Mrs Crosscapel, and the two servants, for the purpose of getting such further information as was thought desirable. Both the cook and the housemaid had given their month's notice to quit; declining, in the interest of their characters, to remain in a house which had been the scene of a murder. Mr Deluc's nerves led also to his removal; his rest was now disturbed by frightful dreams. He paid the necessary forfeit-money, and left without notice. The first-floor lodger, Mr Barfield, kept his rooms, but obtained leave of absence from his employers, and took refuge with some friends in the country. Miss Mybus alone remained in the parlours. 'When I am comfortable,' the old lady said, 'nothing moves me, at my age. A murder up two pairs of stairs is nearly the same thing as a murder in the next house. Distance, you see, makes all the difference.'

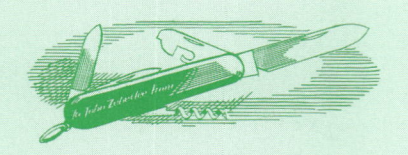

It mattered little to the police what the lodgers did. We had men in plain clothes watching the house night and day. Everybody who went away was privately followed; and the police in the district to which they retired were warned to keep an eye on them, after that. As long as we failed to put Mrs Zebedee's extraordinary statement to any sort of test – to say nothing of having proved unsuccessful, thus far, in tracing the knife to its purchaser – we were bound to let no person living under Mrs Crosscapel's roof, on the night of the murder, slip through our fingers.

4

In a fortnight more, Mrs Zebedee had sufficiently recovered to make the necessary statement – after the preliminary caution addressed to persons in such cases. The surgeon had no hesitation, now, in reporting her to be a sane woman.

Her station in life had been domestic service. She had lived for four years in her last place as lady's-maid, with a family residing in Dorsetshire. The one objection to her had been the occasional infirmity of sleep-walking, which made it necessary that one of the other female servants should sleep in the same room, with the door locked and the key under her pillow. In all other respects the lady's-maid was described by her mistress as 'a perfect treasure'.

In the last six months of her service, a young man named John Zebedee entered the house (with a written character) as footman. He soon fell in love with the nice little lady's-maid, and she heartily returned the feeling. They might have waited for years before they were in a pecuniary position to marry, but for the death of Zebedee's uncle, who left him a little fortune of two thousand pounds. They were now, for persons in their station, rich enough to please themselves; and they were married from the house in which they had served together, the little daughters of the family showing their affection for Mrs Zebedee by acting as her bridesmaids.

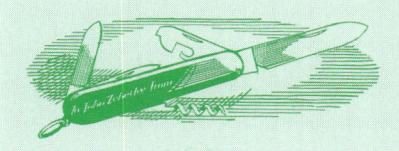

The young husband was a careful man. He decided to employ his small capital to the best advantage, by sheep-farming in Australia. His wife made no objection; she was ready to go wherever John went.

Accordingly they spent their short honeymoon in London, so as to see for themselves the vessel in which their passage was to be taken. They went to Mrs Crosscapel's lodging-house because Zebedee's uncle had always stayed there when he was in London. Ten days were to pass before the day of embarkation arrived. This gave the young couple a welcome holiday, and a prospect of amusing themselves to their hearts' content among the sights and shows of the great city.

On their first evening in London they went to the theatre. They were both accustomed to the fresh air of the country, and they felt half stifled by the heat and the gas. However, they were so pleased with an amusement which was new to them that they went to another theatre on the next evening. On this second occasion, John Zebedee found the heat unendurable. They left the theatre, and got back to their lodgings towards ten o'clock.

Let the rest be told in the words used by Mrs Zebedee herself. She said:

'We sat talking for a little while in our room, and John's headache got worse and worse. I persuaded him to go to bed, and I put out the candle (the fire giving sufficient light to undress by), so that he might the sooner fall asleep. But he was too restless to sleep. He asked me to read him something. Books always made him drowsy at the best of times.

'I had not myself begun to undress. So I lit the candle again, and I opened the only book I had. John had noticed it at the railway bookstall by the name of *The World of Sleep*. He used to joke with me about my being a sleep-walker; and he said, "Here's something that's sure to interest you" – and he made me a present of the book.

'Before I had read to him for more than half an hour he was fast asleep. Not feeling that way inclined, I went on reading to myself.

'The book did indeed interest me. There was one terrible story which took a hold on my mind – the story of a man who stabbed his own wife in a sleep-walking dream. I thought of putting down my book after that, and then changed my mind again and went on. The next chapters were not so interesting; they were full of learned accounts of why we fall asleep, and what our brains do in that state, and such like. It ended in my falling asleep, too, in my armchair by the fireside.

'I don't know what o'clock it was when I went to sleep. I don't know how long I slept, or whether I dreamed or not. The candle and the fire had both burned out, and it was pitch dark when I woke. I can't even say why I woke – unless it was the coldness of the room.

'There was a spare candle on the chimney-piece. I found the match-box, and got a light. Then, for the first time, I turned round towards the bed; and I saw—'

She had seen the dead body of her husband, murdered while she was unconsciously at his side – and she fainted, poor creature, at the bare remembrance of it.

The proceedings were adjourned. She received every possible care and attention; the chaplain looking after her welfare as well as the surgeon.

I have said nothing of the evidence of the landlady and the servants. It was taken as a mere formality. What little they knew proved nothing against Mrs Zebedee. The police made no discoveries that supported her first frantic accusation of herself. Her master and mistress, where she had been last in service, spoke of her in the highest terms. We were at a complete deadlock.

It had been thought best not to surprise Mr Deluc, as yet, by citing him as a witness. The action of the law was, however, hurried in this case by a private communication received from the chaplain.

After twice seeing, and speaking with, Mrs Zebedee, the reverend gentleman was persuaded that she had no more to do than himself with the murder of her husband. He did not consider that he was justified in repeating a confidential communication – he would only recommend that Mr Deluc should be summoned to appear at the next examination. This advice was followed.

The police had no evidence against Mrs Zebedee when the inquiry was resumed. To assist the ends of justice she was now put into the witness-box. The discovery of her murdered husband, when she woke in the small hours of the morning, was passed over as rapidly as possible. Only three questions of importance were put to her.

First, the knife was produced. Had she ever seen it in her husband's possession? Never. Did she know anything about it? Nothing whatever.

Secondly: Did she, or did her husband, lock the bedroom door when they returned from the theatre? No. Did she afterwards lock the door herself? No.

Thirdly: Had she any sort of reason to give for supposing that she had murdered her husband in a sleep-walking dream? No reason, except that she was beside herself at the time, and the book put the thought into her head.

After this the other witnesses were sent out of court. The motive for the chaplain's communication now appeared. Mrs Zebedee was asked if anything unpleasant had occurred between Mr Deluc and herself.

Yes. He had caught her alone on the stairs at the lodging-house; had presumed to make love to her; and had carried the insult still further by attempting to kiss her. She had slapped his face, and had declared that her husband should know of it, if his misconduct was repeated. He was in a furious rage at having his face slapped; and he said to her: 'Madam, you may live to regret this.'

After consultation, and at the request of our Inspector, it was decided to keep Mr Deluc in ignorance of Mrs Zebedee's statement for the present. When the witnesses were recalled, he gave the same evidence which he had already given to the Inspector – and he was then asked if he knew anything of the knife. He looked at it without any guilty signs in his face, and swore that he had never seen it until that moment. The resumed inquiry ended, and still nothing had been discovered.

But we kept an eye on Mr Deluc. Our next effort was to try if we could associate him with the purchase of the knife.

Here again (there really did seem to be a sort of fatality in this case) we reached no useful result. It was easy enough to find out the wholesale cutlers, who had manufactured the knife at Sheffield, by the mark on the blade. But they made tens of thousands of such knives, and disposed of them to retail dealers all over Great Britain – to say nothing of foreign parts. As to finding out the person who had engraved the imperfect inscription (without knowing where, or by whom, the knife had been purchased) we might as well have looked for the proverbial needle in the bundle of hay. Our last resource was to have the knife photographed, with the inscribed side uppermost, and to send copies to every police-station in the kingdom.

At the same time we reckoned up Mr Deluc – I mean that we made investigations into his past life – on the chance that he and the murdered man might have known each other, and might have had a quarrel, or a rivalry about a woman, on some former occasion. No such discovery rewarded us.

We found Deluc to have led a dissipated life, and to have mixed with very bad company. But he had kept out of reach of the law. A man may be a profligate vagabond; may insult a lady; may say threatening things to her, in the first stinging sensation of having his face slapped – but it doesn't follow from these blots on his character that he has murdered her husband in the dead of the night.

Once more, then, when we were called upon to report ourselves, we had no evidence to produce. The photographs failed to discover the owner of the knife, and to explain its interrupted inscription. Poor Mrs Zebedee was allowed to go back to her friends, on entering into her own recognizance to appear again if called upon. Articles in the newspapers began to enquire how many more murderers would succeed in baffling the police. The authorities at the Treasury offered a reward of a hundred pounds for the necessary information. And the weeks passed, and nobody claimed the reward.

Our Inspector was not a man to be easily beaten. More enquiries and examinations followed. It is needless to say anything about them. We were defeated – and there, so far as the police and the public were concerned, was an end of it.

The assassination of the poor young husband soon passed out of notice, like other undiscovered murders. One obscure person only was foolish enough, in his leisure hours, to persist in trying to solve the problem of Who Killed Zebedee? He felt that he might rise to the highest position in the police-force if he succeeded where his elders and betters had failed – and he held to his own little ambition, though everybody laughed at him. In plain English, I was the man.

5

Without meaning it, I have told my story ungratefully.

There were two persons who saw nothing ridiculous in my resolution to continue the investigation, single-handed. One of them was Miss Mybus; and the other was the cook, Priscilla Thurlby.

Mentioning the lady first, Miss Mybus was indignant at the resigned manner in which the police accepted their defeat. She was a little bright-eyed wiry woman; and she spoke her mind freely.

'This comes home to me,' she said. 'Just look back for a year or two. I can call to mind two cases of persons found murdered in London – and the assassins have never been traced. I am a person too; and I ask myself if my turn is not coming next. You're a nice-looking fellow – and I like your pluck and perseverance. Come here as often as you think right; and say you are my visitor, if they make any difficulty about letting you in. One thing more! I have nothing particular to do, and I am no fool. Here, in the parlours, I see everybody who comes into the house or goes out of the house. Leave me your address – I may get some information for you yet.'

With the best intentions, Miss Mybus found no opportunity of helping me. Of the two, Priscilla Thurlby seemed more likely to be of use.

In the first place, she was sharp and active, and (not having succeeded in getting another situation as yet) was mistress of her own movements.

In the second place, she was a woman I could trust. Before she left home to try domestic service in London, the parson of her native parish gave her a written testimonial, of which I append a copy. Thus it ran:

> 'I gladly recommend Priscilla Thurlby for any respectable employment which she may be competent to undertake. Her father and mother are infirm old people, who have lately suffered a diminution of their income; and they have a younger daughter to maintain. Rather than be a burden on her parents, Priscilla goes to London to find domestic employment, and to devote her earnings to the assistance of her father and mother. This circumstance speaks for itself. I have known the family many years; and I only regret that I have no vacant place in my own household which I can offer to this good girl.
>
> '(Signed)
> HENRY DERRINGTON, Rector of Roth.'

After reading those words, I could safely ask Priscilla to help me in reopening the mysterious murder case to some good purpose.

My notion was that the proceedings of the persons in Mrs Crosscapel's house, had not been closely enough enquired into yet. By way of continuing the investigation, I asked Priscilla if she could tell me anything which associated the housemaid with Mr Deluc. She was unwilling to answer. 'I may be casting suspicion on an innocent person,' she said. 'Besides, I was for so short a time the housemaid's fellow servant—'

'You slept in the same room with her,' I remarked; 'and you had opportunities of observing her conduct towards the lodgers. If they had asked you, at the examination, what I now ask, you would have answered as an honest woman.'

To this argument she yielded. I heard from her certain particulars which threw a new light on Mr Deluc, and on the case generally. On that information I acted. It was slow work, owing to the claims on me of my regular duties; but with Priscilla's help, I steadily advanced towards the end I had in view.

Besides this, I owed another obligation to Mrs Crosscapel's nice-looking cook. The confession must be made sooner or later – and I may as well make it now. I first knew what love was, thanks to Priscilla. I had delicious kisses, thanks to Priscilla. And, when I asked if she would marry me, she didn't say No. She looked, I must own, a little sadly, and she said: 'How can two such poor people as we are ever hope to marry?' To this I answered: 'It won't be long before I lay my hand on the clue which my Inspector has failed to find. I shall be in a position to marry you, my dear, when that time comes.'

At our next meeting we spoke of her parents. I was now her promised husband. Judging by what I had heard of the proceedings of other people in my position, it seemed to be only right that I should be made known to her father and mother. She entirely agreed with me; and she wrote home that day, to tell them to expect us at the end of the week.

I took my turn of night duty, and so gained my liberty for the greater part of the next day. I dressed myself in plain clothes, and we took our tickets on the railway for Yateland, being the nearest station to the village in which Priscilla's parents lived.

6

The train stopped, as usual, at the big town of Waterbank. Supporting herself by her needle, while she was still unprovided with a situation, Priscilla had been at work late in the night – she was tired and thirsty. I left the carriage to get her some soda-water. The stupid girl in the refreshment room failed to pull the cork out of the bottle and refused to let me help her. She took a corkscrew, and used it crookedly. I lost all patience, and snatched the bottle out of her hand. Just as I drew the cork, the bell rang on the platform. I only waited to pour the soda-water into a glass – but the train was moving as I left the refreshment-room. The porters stopped me when I tried to jump on to the step of the carriage. I was left behind.

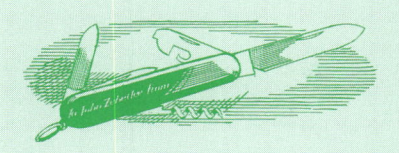

As soon as I had recovered my temper, I looked at the timetable. We had reached Waterbank at five minutes past one. By good luck, the next train was due at forty-four minutes past one, and arrived at Yateland (the next station) ten minutes afterwards. I could only hope that Priscilla would look at the timetable too, and wait for me. If I had attempted to walk the distance between the two places, I should have lost time instead of saving it. The interval before me was not very long; I occupied it in looking over the town.

Speaking with all due respect to the inhabitants, Waterbank (to other people) is a dull place. I went up one street and down another – and stopped to look at a shop which struck me; not from anything in itself, but because it was the only shop in the street with the shutters closed.

A bill was posted on the shutters, announcing that the place was to let. The outgoing tradesman's name and business, announced in the customary painted letters, ran thus: – *James Wycomb, Cutler, etc.*

For the first time, it occurred to me that we had forgotten an obstacle in our way, when we distributed our photographs of the knife. We had none of us remembered that a certain proportion of cutlers might be placed, by circumstances, out of our reach – either by retiring from business or by becoming bankrupt. I always carried a copy of the photograph about me; and I thought to myself, 'Here is the ghost of a chance of tracing the knife to Mr Deluc!'

The shop door was opened, after I had twice rung the bell, by an old man, very dirty and very deaf. He said: 'You had better go upstairs, and speak to Mr Scorrier – top of the house.'

I put my lips to the old fellow's ear-trumpet, and asked who Mr Scorrier was.

'Brother-in-law to Mr Wycomb. Mr Wycomb's dead. If you want to buy the business apply to Mr Scorrier.'

Receiving that reply, I went upstairs, and found Mr Scorrier engaged in engraving a brass door-plate. He was a middle-aged man, with a cadaverous face and dim eyes. After the necessary apologies, I produced my photograph.

'May I ask, sir, if you know anything of the inscription on that knife?' I said.

He took his magnifying glass to look at it.

'This is curious,' he remarked quietly. 'I remember the queer name – Zebedee. Yes, sir; I did the engraving, as far as it goes. I wonder what prevented me from finishing it?'

The name of Zebedee, and the unfinished inscription on the knife, had appeared in every English newspaper. He took the matter so coolly, that I was doubtful how to interpret his answer. Was it possible that he had not seen the account of the murder? Or was he an accomplice with prodigious powers of self-control?

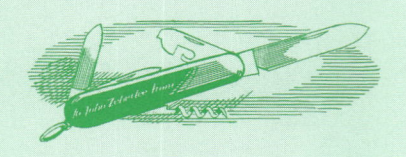

'Excuse me,' I said, 'do you read the newspapers?'

'Never! My eyesight is failing me. I abstain from reading, in the interests of my occupation.'

'Have you not heard the name of Zebedee mentioned – particularly by people who do read the newspapers?'

'Very likely; but I didn't attend to it. When the day's work is done, I take my walk. Then I have my supper, my drop of grog, and my pipe. Then I go to bed. A dull existence you think, I dare say! I had a miserable life, sir, when I was young. A bare subsistence, and a little rest, before the last perfect rest in the grave – that is all I want. The world has gone by me long ago. So much the better.'

The poor man spoke honestly. I was ashamed of having doubted him. I returned to the subject of the knife.

'Do you know where it was purchased, and by whom?' I asked.

'My memory is not so good as it was,' he said; 'but I have got something by me that helps it.'

He took from a cupboard a dirty old scrapbook. Strips of paper, with writing on them, were pasted on the pages, as well as I could see. He turned to an index, or table of contents, and opened a page. Something like a flash of life showed itself on his dismal face.

'Ha! now I remember,' he said. 'The knife was bought of my late brother-in-law, in the shop downstairs. It all comes back to me, sir. A person in a state of frenzy burst into this very room, and snatched the knife away from me, when I was only half way through the inscription!'

I felt that I was now close on discovery. 'May I see what it is that has assisted your memory?' I asked.

'Oh yes. You must know, sir, I live by engraving inscriptions and addresses, and I paste in this book the manuscript instructions which I receive, with marks of my own on the margin. For one thing, they serve as a reference to new customers. And for another thing, they do certainly help my memory.'

He turned the book towards me, and pointed to a slip of paper which occupied the lower half of a page.

I read the complete inscription, intended for the knife that killed Zebedee, and written as follows:

'To John Zebedee. From Priscilla Thurlby.'

7

I declare that it is impossible for me to describe what I felt, when Priscilla's name confronted me like a written confession of guilt. How long it was before I recovered myself in some degree, I cannot say. The only thing I can clearly call to mind is, that I frightened the poor engraver.

My first desire was to get possession of the manuscript inscription. I told him I was a policeman, and summoned him to assist me in the discovery of a crime. I even offered him money. He drew back from my hand. 'You shall have it for nothing,' he said, 'if you will only go away and never come here again.' He tried to cut it out of the page – but his trembling hands were helpless. I cut it out myself, and attempted to thank him. He wouldn't hear me. 'Go away!' he said, 'I don't like the look of you.'

It may be here objected that I ought not to have felt so sure as I did of the woman's guilt, until I had got more evidence against her. The knife might have been stolen from her, supposing she was the person who had snatched it out of the engraver's hands, and might have been afterwards used by the thief to commit the murder. All very true. But I never had a moment's doubt in my own mind, from the time when I read the damnable line in the engraver's book.

I went back to the railway without any plan in my head. The train by which I had proposed to follow her had left Waterbank. The next train that arrived was for London. I took my place in it – still without any plan in my head.

At Charing Cross a friend met me. He said, 'You're looking miserably ill. Come and have a drink.'

I went with him. The liquor was what I really wanted; it strung me up, and cleared my head. He went his way, and I went mine. In a little while more, I determined what I would do.

In the first place, I decided to resign my situation in the police, from a motive which will presently appear. In the second place, I took a bed at a public house. She would no doubt return to London, and she would go to my lodgings to find out why I had broken my appointment. To bring to justice the one woman whom I had dearly loved was too cruel a duty for a poor creature like me. I preferred leaving the police-force. On the other hand, if she and I met before time had helped me to control myself, I had a horrid fear that I might turn murderer next, and kill her then and there. The wretch had not only all but misled me into marrying her, but also into charging the innocent housemaid with being concerned in the murder.

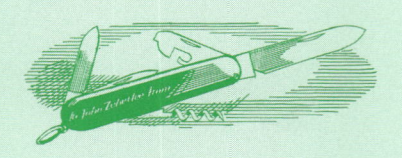

The same night I hit on a way of clearing up such doubts as still harassed my mind. I wrote to the Rector of Roth, informing him that I was engaged to marry her, and asking if he would tell me (in consideration of my position) what her former relations might have been with the person named John Zebedee.

By return of post I got this reply: –

Sir, – Under the circumstances, I think I am bound to tell you confidentially what the friends and well-wishers of Priscilla have kept secret, for her sake.

Zebedee was in service in this neighbourhood. I am sorry to say it, of a man who has come to such a miserable end – but his behaviour to Priscilla proves him to have been a vicious and heartless wretch. They were engaged – and, I add with indignation, he tried to seduce her under a promise of marriage. Her virtue resisted him, and he pretended to be ashamed of himself. The banns were published in my church. On the next day Zebedee disappeared, and cruelly deserted her. He was a capable servant; and I believe he got another place. I leave you to imagine what the poor girl suffered under the outrage inflicted on her. Going to London, with my recommendation, she answered the first advertisement that she saw, and was unfortunate enough to begin her career in domestic service in the very lodging-house, to which (as I gather from the newspaper report of the murder) the man Zebedee took the person whom he married, after deserting Priscilla. Be assured that you are about to unite yourself to an excellent girl, and accept my best wishes for your happiness.

It was plain from this that neither the rector nor the parents and friends knew anything of the purchase of the knife. The one miserable man who knew the truth, was the man who had asked her to be his wife.

I owed it to myself – at least so it seemed to me – not to let it be supposed that I, too, had meanly deserted her. Dreadful as the prospect was, I felt that I must see her once more, and for the last time.

She was at work when I went into her room. As I opened the door she started to her feet. Her cheeks reddened, and her eyes flashed with anger. I stepped forward – and she saw my face. My face silenced her.

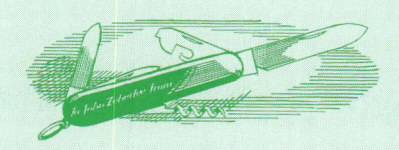

I spoke in the fewest words I could find.

'I have been to the cutler's shop at Waterbank,' I said. "There is the unfinished inscription on the knife, completed in your handwriting. I could hang you by a word. God forgive me – I can't say the word.'

Her bright complexion turned to a dreadful clay-colour. Her eyes were fixed and staring, like the eyes of a person in a fit. She stood before me, still and silent. Without saying more, I dropped the inscription into the fire. Without saying more, I left her.

I never saw her again.

8

But I heard from her a few days later.

The letter has been long since burnt. I wish I could have forgotten it as well. It sticks to my memory. If I die with my senses about me, Priscilla's letter will be my last recollection on earth.

In substance it repeated what the rector had already told me. Further, it informed me that she had bought the knife as a keep-sake for Zebedee, in place of a similar knife which he had lost. On the Saturday, she made the purchase, and left it to be engraved. On the Sunday, the banns were put up. On the Monday, she was deserted; and she snatched the knife from the table while the engraver was at work.

She only knew that Zebedee had added a new sting to the insult inflicted on her, when he arrived at the lodgings with his wife. Her duties as cook kept her in the kitchen – and Zebedee never discovered that she was in the house. I still remember the last lines of her confession:

> *The devil entered into me when I tried their door, on my way up to bed, and found it unlocked, and listened awhile, and peeped in. I saw them by the dying light of the candle – one asleep on the bed, the other*

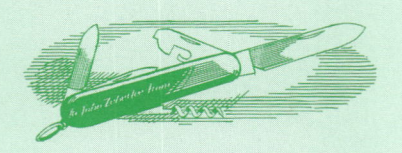

asleep by the fireside. I had the knife in my hand, and the thought came to me to do it, so that they might hang her for the murder. I couldn't take the knife out again, when I had done it. Mind this! I did really like you – I didn't say Yes, because you could hardly hang your own wife, if you found out who killed Zebedee.

* * *

Since that past time I have never heard again of Priscilla Thurlby; I don't know whether she is living or dead. Many people may think I deserve to be hanged myself for not having given her up to the gallows. They may, perhaps, be disappointed when they see this confession, and hear that I have died decently in my bed. I don't blame them. I am a penitent sinner. I wish all merciful Christians goodbye for ever.

Reading the Charles Dickens

The next text, *A Confession Found in a Prison in the Time of Charles the Second*, by Charles Dickens, is one of the author's many short pieces involving the supernatural and was particularly admired by Edgar Allan Poe, the great American writer of supernatural and horror stories. It was first published in a weekly magazine in 1840. Although Dickens' novels and stories often contain detailed descriptions of everyday life and situations, he was always fascinated by the bizarre and the unusual, and by the fear and terror which could lurk behind the apparently normal.

This piece is similar to the previous story in being the confession of a man about to die, and who wishes to clear his conscience of a crime. You may well feel less **sympathy** for this narrator than for Mr Policeman, however!

While you read this text, think about:

- how the character of the narrator differs from Collins' policeman; how you feel towards him and why
- how Dickens shows convincingly the gradual build-up of the narrator's wish to kill his adopted child

- how Dickens uses references to the natural world to heighten the emotion involved in the description of the boy's murder
- whether the plot is more believable than that of the Collins' story, and why
- the effect of the final paragraph on your feelings towards the narrator, and how Dickens' style contributes towards this.

by Charles Dickens

A Confession Found in a Prison in the Time of Charles the Second

I HELD A LIEUTENANT'S COMMISSION in His Majesty's army and served abroad in the campaigns of 1677 and 1678. The treaty of Nimeguen being concluded, I returned home, and retiring from the service withdrew to a small estate lying a few miles east of London, which I had recently acquired in right of my wife.

This is the last night I have to live, and I will set down the naked truth without disguise. I was never a brave man, and had always been from my childhood of a secret sullen distrustful nature. I speak of myself as if I had passed from the world, for while I write this my grave is digging and my name is written in the black book of death.

Soon after my return to England, my only brother was seized with mortal illness. This circumstance gave me slight or no pain, for since we had been men we had associated but very little together. He was open-hearted and generous, handsomer than I, more accomplished, and generally beloved. Those who sought my acquaintance abroad or at home because they were friends of his, seldom attached themselves to me long, and would usually say in our first conversation that they were surprised to find two brothers so unlike in their manners and appearance. It was my habit to lead them on to this avowal, for I knew what comparisons they must draw between us, and having a rankling envy in my heart, I sought to justify it to myself.

We had married two sisters. This additional tie between us, as it may appear to some, only estranged us the more. His wife knew me well. I never struggled with any secret jealousy or gall when she was present but that woman knew it as well as I did. I never raised my eyes at such times but I found hers fixed upon me; I never bent them on the ground or looked another way, but I felt that she overlooked me always. It was an inexpressible relief to me when we quarrelled, and a greater relief still when I heard abroad that she was dead. It seems to me now as if some strange and terrible foreshadowing of what has happened since, must have hung over us then. I was afraid of her, she haunted me, her fixed and steady look comes back upon me now like the memory of a dark dream and makes my blood run cold.

She died shortly after giving birth to a child – a boy. When my brother knew that all hope of his own recovery was past, he called my wife to his bed-side and confided this orphan, a child of four years old, to her protection. He bequeathed to him all the property he had, and willed that in case of the child's death it should pass to my wife as the only acknowledgement he could make her for her care and love. He exchanged a few brotherly words with me deploring our long separation, and being exhausted, fell into a slumber from which he never awoke.

We had no children, and as there had been a strong affection between the sisters, and my wife had almost supplied the place of a mother to this boy, she loved him as if he had been her own. The child was ardently attached to her; but he was his mother's image in face and spirit and always mistrusted me.

I can scarcely fix the date when the feeling first came upon me, but I soon began to be uneasy when this child was by. I never roused myself from some moody train of thought but I marked him looking at me: not with mere childish wonder, but with something of the purpose and meaning that I had so often noted in his mother. It was no effort of my fancy, founded on close resemblance of feature and expression. I never could look the boy down. He feared me, but seemed by some instinct to despise me while he did so; and even when he drew back beneath my gaze – as he would when we were alone, to get nearer to the door – he would keep his bright eyes upon me still.

Perhaps I hide the truth from myself, but I do not think that when this began, I meditated to do him any wrong. I may have thought how serviceable his inheritance would be to us, and may have wished him dead, but I believe I had no thought of compassing his death. Neither did the idea come upon me at once, but by very slow degrees, presenting itself at first in dim shapes at a very great distance, as men may think of an earthquake or the last day – then drawing nearer and nearer and losing something of its horror and improbability – then coming to be part and parcel, nay nearly the whole sum and substance of my daily thoughts, and resolving itself into a question of means and safety; not of doing or abstaining from the deed.

While this was going on within me, I never could bear that the child should see me looking at him, and yet I was under a fascination which made it a kind of business with me to contemplate his slight and fragile figure and think how easily it might be done. Sometimes I would steal upstairs and watch him as he slept, but usually I hovered in the garden near the window of the room in which he learnt his little tasks, and there as he sat upon a low seat beside my wife, I would peer at him for hours together from behind a tree: starting like the guilty wretch I was at every rustling of a leaf, and still gliding back to look and start again.

Hard by our cottage, but quite out of sight, and (if there were any wind astir) of hearing too, was a deep sheet of water. I spent days in shaping with my pocket-knife a rough model of a boat, which I finished at last and dropped in the child's way. Then I withdrew to a secret place which he must pass if he stole away alone to swim this bauble, and lurked there for his coming. He came neither that day nor the next, though I waited from noon till nightfall. I was sure that I had him in my net for I had heard him prattling of the toy, and knew that in his infant pleasure he kept it by his side in bed. I felt no weariness or fatigue, but waited patiently, and on the third day he passed me, running joyously along, with his silken hair streaming in the wind and he singing – God have mercy upon me! – singing a merry ballad – who could hardly lisp the words.

I stole down after him, creeping under certain shrubs which grow in that place, and none but devils know with what terror I, a full-grown man, tracked the footsteps of that baby as he approached the water's brink. I was close upon him, had sunk upon my knee and raised my hand to thrust him in, when he saw my shadow in the stream and turned him round.

His mother's ghost was looking from his eyes. The sun burst forth from behind a cloud: it shone in the bright sky, the glistening earth, the clear water, the sparkling drops of rain upon the leaves. There were eyes in everything. The whole great universe of light was there to see the murder done. I know not what he said; he came of bold and manly blood, and child as he was, he did not crouch or fawn upon me. I heard him cry that he would try to love me – not that he did – and then I saw him running back towards the house. The next I saw was my own sword naked in my hand and he lying at my feet stark dead – dabbled here and there with blood but otherwise no different from what I had seen him in his sleep – in the same attitude too, with his cheek resting upon his little hand.

I took him in my arms and laid him – very gently now that he was dead – in a thicket. My wife was from home that day and would not return until the next. Our bed-room window, the only sleeping room on that side of the house, was but a few feet from the ground, and I resolved to descend from it at night and bury him in the garden. I had no thought that I had failed in my design, no thought that the water would be dragged and nothing found, that the money must now lie waste since I must encourage the idea that the child was lost or stolen. All my thoughts were bound up and knotted together, in the one absorbing necessity of hiding what I had done.

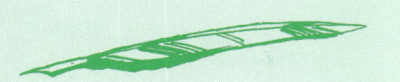

How I felt when they came to tell me that the child was missing, when I ordered scouts in all directions, when I gasped and trembled at everyone's approach, no tongue can tell or mind of man conceive. I buried him that night. When I parted the boughs and looked into the dark thicket, there was a glow-worm shining like the visible spirit of God upon the murdered child. I glanced down into his grave when I had placed him there and still it gleamed upon his breast: an eye of fire looking up to Heaven in supplication to the stars that watched me at my work.

I had to meet my wife, and break the news, and give her hope that the child would soon be found. All this I did – with some appearance, I suppose, of being sincere, for I was the object of no suspicion. This done, I sat at the bed-room window all day long and watched the spot where the dreadful secret lay.

It was in a piece of ground which had been dug up to be newly turfed, and which I had chosen on that account as the traces of my spade were less likely to attract attention. The men who laid down the grass must have thought me mad. I called to them continually to expedite their work, ran out and worked beside them, trod down the turf with my feet, and hurried them with frantic eagerness. They had finished their task before night, and then I thought myself comparatively safe.

I slept – not as men do who wake refreshed and cheerful, but I did sleep, passing from vague and shadowy dreams of being hunted down, to visions of the plot of grass, through which now a hand and now a foot and now the head itself was starting out. At this point I always woke and stole to the window to make sure that it was not really so. That done I crept to bed again, and thus I spent the night in fits and starts, getting up and lying down full twenty times and dreaming the same dream over and over again – which was far worse than lying awake, for every dream had a whole night's suffering of its own. Once I thought the child was alive and that I had never tried to kill him. To wake from that dream was the most dreadful agony of all.

The next day I sat at the window again, never once taking my eyes from the place, which, although it was covered by the grass, was as plain to me – its shape, its size, its depth, its jagged sides, and all – as if it had been open to the light of day. When a servant walked across it, I felt as if he must sink in; when he had passed I looked to see that his feet had not worn the edges. If a bird lighted there, I was in terror lest by some tremendous interposition it should be instrumental in the discovery; if a breath of air sighed across it, to me it whispered murder. There was not a sight or sound how ordinary mean or unimportant soever, but was fraught with fear. And in this state of ceaseless watching I spent three days.

On the fourth, there came to the gate one who had served with me abroad, accompanied by a brother officer of his whom I had never seen. I felt that I could not bear to be out of sight of the place. It was a summer evening, and I bade my people take a table and a flask of wine into the garden. Then I sat down *with my chair upon the grave*, and being assured that nobody could disturb it now, without my knowledge, tried to drink and talk.

They hoped that my wife was well – that she was not obliged to keep her chamber – that they had not frightened her away. What could I do but tell them with a faltering tongue about the child? The officer whom I did not know was a down-looking man and kept his eyes upon the ground while I was speaking. Even that terrified me! I could not divest myself of the idea that he saw something there which caused him to suspect the truth. I asked him hurriedly if he supposed that – and stopped. 'That the child had been murdered?' said he, looking mildly at me. 'Oh, no! what could a man gain by murdering a poor child?' *I* could have told him what a man gained by such a deed, no one better, but I held my peace and shivered as with an ague.

Mistaking my emotion they were endeavouring to cheer me with the hope that the boy would certainly be found – great cheer that was for me – when we heard a low deep howl, and presently there sprung over the wall two great dogs, who bounding into the garden repeated the baying sound we had heard before.

'Blood-hounds!' cried my visitors.

What need to tell me that! I had never seen one of that kind in all my life, but I knew what they were and for what purpose they had come. I grasped the elbows of my chair, and neither spoke nor moved.

'They are of the genuine breed,' said the man whom I had known abroad, 'and being out for exercise have no doubt escaped from their keeper.'

Both he and his friend turned to look at the dogs, who with their noses to the ground moved restlessly about, running to and fro, and up and down, and across, and round in circles, careering about like wild things, and all this time taking no notice of us, but ever and again lifting their heads and repeating the yell we had heard already, then dropping their noses to the ground again and tracking earnestly here and there. They now began to snuff the earth more eagerly than they had done yet, and although they were still very restless, no longer beat about in such wide circuits, but kept near to one spot, and constantly diminished the distance between themselves and me.

At last they came up close to the great chair on which I sat, and raising their frightful howl once more, tried to tear away the wooden rails that kept them from the ground beneath. I saw how I looked, in the faces of the two who were with me.

'They scent some prey,' said they, both together.

'They scent no prey!' cried I.

'In Heaven's name move,' said the one I knew, very earnestly, 'or you will be torn to pieces.'

'Let them tear me limb from limb, I'll never leave this place!' cried I. 'Are dogs to hurry men to shameful deaths? Hew them down, cut them in pieces.'

'There is some foul mystery here!' said the officer whom I did not know, drawing his sword. 'In King Charles's name assist me to secure this man.'

They both set upon me and forced me away, though I fought and bit and caught at them like a madman. After a struggle they got me quietly between them, and then, my God! I saw the angry dogs tearing at the earth and throwing it up into the air like water.

What more have I to tell? That I fell upon my knees and with chattering teeth confessed the truth and prayed to be forgiven. That I have since denied and now confess to it again. That I have been tried for the crime, found guilty, and sentenced. That I have not the courage to anticipate my doom or to bear up manfully against it. That I have no compassion, no consolation, no hope, no friend. That my wife has happily lost for the time those faculties which would enable her to know my misery or hers. That I am alone in this stone dungeon with my evil spirit, and that I die to-morrow!

Reading the Alan Bennett

The final piece in this chapter is a complete television script by Alan Bennett, *The Outside Dog*. Written in 1998, it reveals a situation similar in some ways to those in the three previous texts. Marjory, the only character we ever see, realises that her husband is a serial murderer but this hardly seems to deflect her from her obsession with housework or her dislike of Tina, the dog who is ultimately responsible for the husband being acquitted. Because this is a television script, and particularly because it is a monologue, it has the appropriate genre qualities noted earlier. You, the viewer or reader, have to think between the lines to work out just what is going on in Marjory's mind and what her husband, Stuart, has actually done.

If possible, watch this play on video. If you cannot, read the words aloud so that you can hear their effect in building up Marjory's character and situation. As you watch or listen, think about:

- when it is you realise, and why, that Stuart is the murderer and that Marjory knows
- how the script influences the views you form about off-stage characters such as Mrs Catchpole, Stuart's mother, the police and the reporters
- the ideas or attitudes Bennett conveys about Marjory
- what makes the language or style seem realistic
- how this script uses particular genre qualities effectively.

The Outside Dog
by Alan Bennett

Afternoon. The kitchen. Against a blank, wallpapered wall. One chair. Possibly some artificial flowers. Similar settings throughout.

I'd be the same if it was a cat. Because they make as much mess as dogs. Only cats you can be allergic to, so people make allowances. And flowers, of course, some people. Only we don't have flowers. Well, we do but they're all washable. I just think it spies on me, that tongue lolling out.

He took the van over to Rawdon last night. Said it was Rawdon anyway. Doing something or other, fly-tipping probably. Takes Tina which was a relief from the woof-woofing plus it gave me a chance to swill.

I'd had Mrs Catchpole opposite banging on the door in the afternoon saying she was going to the council because it wanted putting down. I said, 'I agree.' She said, 'I'm getting a petition up.' I said, 'Well, when you do, fetch it across because I'll be the first signatory.' I hate the flaming dog. Of course she doesn't do it with him. Never makes a muff when he's around.

He comes in after midnight, puts his clothes in the washer. I said to him last week, 'Why don't you do your washing at a cultivated hour?' He said, 'You're lucky I do it at all.' Still, at least the washer's in the shed. I shouted down, 'That dog's not inside is she?' He said, 'No. Get to sleep.' Which I was doing only when he comes up he has nothing on. He leaves it a bit then slides over to my side and starts carrying on.

Found a dog hair or two on the carpet this morning so that meant another shampooing job. I only did it last week. This shampoo's got air-freshener in, plus a disinfectant apparently.

Non-stop down at the yard since they started killing off the cows, so when he comes in this dinner-time he wants to eat straight off. Swills his boots under the outside tap and he's coming in like that. I said, 'Stuart. You know the rules. Take them off.' He said, 'There's no time.' So I said, 'Well, if there's not time you'll have it on the step.' Sits there eating and feeding Tina. She licks his boots. Literally. I suppose it's with him coming straight from the slaughterhouse.

Seems to have lost another anorak, this one fur-lined.

Fade

She comes up this afternoon, his mother, all dolled up. Says, 'You've got this place nice. How do you manage with our Stuart?' I said, 'I've got him trained.' She said, 'He's not trained when he comes down our house.' 'Well,' I said, 'perhaps he doesn't get the encouragement.' She said, 'I don't like it when they're too tidy. It's not natural.'

Not natural at their house. They've no culture at all. First time I went down there they were having their dinner and there was a pan stuck on the table. When it comes to evolution they're scarcely above pig-sty level. And she must be sixty, still dyes her hair, fag in her mouth, big ear-rings. She said, 'You don't mind if I smoke? Or do you want me to sit on the step?'

I gave her a saucer only it didn't do much good, ash all over the shop. She does it on purpose. It had gone five, she said, 'Where is he?' I said, 'Where he generally is at this time of day: slitting some defenceless creature's throat. They're on overtime.'

She went before it got dark. Said she was nervous what with this feller on the loose. Made a fuss of Tina. Remembered her when she was a puppy running round their house. I remember it an' all. Doing its business all up and down, the place stank. It was me that trained Stuart. Me that trained the dog.

Except for the din. Can't train that. Leaves off, of course when he appears. He doesn't believe she does it. I said to him, 'Is it safe for me to go on to the library?' He said, 'Why?' I said, 'There's a lass dead in Wakefield now.' He said, 'You don't cross any waste ground. Take Tina.'

Anyway I didn't go and when he's changed out of his muck and swilled everything off he put on his navy shirt, little chain round his neck and the tan slacks we bought him in Marbella. I brought him a beer in a glass while I had a sherry. Him sat on one side of the fire, me on the other, watching TV with the sound down. I said, 'This is a nice civilised evening.'

Except of course madam gets wind of the fact that we're having a nice time and starts whimpering and whatnot and jumping up outside the window and carries on and carries on until he has to take her out. Gone two hours so I was in bed when he got back.

Comes upstairs without his trousers on. I said, 'What've you done with your slacks?' He said, 'The dog jumped up and got mud on. Anyway it's quite handy isn't it?' I said, 'Why?' He said, 'Why do you think? Move up.'

Lots of shouting and whatnot. I thought in the middle of it, it's a blessing we're detached. 'Sorry about that,' he said when he'd done. 'I get carried away.'

Loudspeaker van came round this afternoon saying the police were going to be coming round. House to house. I was just getting some stuff ready to take to the dry cleaners while it was light still.

Couldn't find his slacks.

Fade

She said, 'Have you any suspicions of anyone in your family?' I said, 'What family? There's only me and him.' He said, 'We can't talk with this dog carrying on. Can't we come inside?' I said, 'You've told people not to open their doors.' She said, 'But we're the police.' I said, 'Well, take your shoes off.'

She's in uniform, he's got a raincoat on. She said, 'We've had complaints about the dog. It's in your print-out.' I said, 'Oh it's the dog, is it? I thought it was the killer you were after.' She said, 'Your hubby says it never barks.' I said, 'When did you talk to him?' She said, 'At his place of employment. These are the dates of the murders. Look at them and tell me whether you can remember where your husband was on any of these dates.' I said, 'He was at home. He's always at home.' She said, 'Our information is he'll sometimes go out.' I said, 'Yes. With the dog. Do you know dogs? They occasionally want to have a jimmy riddle.' She said, 'What about this fly-tipping? His van's been seen.' I said, 'The van's not my province. Though I've shared the back seat with a beast head before now.'

Meanwhile the one in the raincoat's been sitting there saying nothing, looking round, sizing the place up. Suddenly he stands up. 'Can I use the toilet?' I said, 'Now? Well, you'll have to wait while I put a paper down.'

I took him upstairs and waited outside. He says, 'I can't do it with you listening.' So I came downstairs again. And she says, 'He's got a funny bladder.'

'One last question. Have you noticed anything out of the ordinary about your husband stroke boy friend stroke father stroke son ... well, that's husband in your case... over the last six months?' 'Like what?' 'Blood on his clothes?' I said, 'There's always blood. He's a slaughterman. Only you won't find any in here. And you won't find any outside. He swills it off.' I said, 'Your friend's taking his time.' She said, 'Men have problems with their water. I've an idea he has an appliance.'

When eventually he comes down he says, 'You keep the place tidy.' I said, 'I used to be a teacher.' He said, 'What did you teach?' I said, 'Children.' He said,

'Do you have any?' I said, 'Does it look like it?'

As they're going Mother Catchpole opposite is stood in the road and shouts across, 'I've got something to tell you.' So the girl goes over and has a word. Comes back. 'Nothing,' she says. 'Just the flaming dog.' 'Nobody listens to me,' she's shouting, 'I've had a depression with that dog.'

I shut the door. When I went upstairs to wipe round the toilet I saw he'd moved one or two ornaments. Nothing else that I could see.

When his lordship came in I said, 'You never told me they'd been to your work.' He said, 'It was routine. I've tipped on one of the sites where they found one of them.' I said, 'Did you find that ticket?' He said, 'What ticket?' 'For the dry cleaners. The tan slacks.' He said, 'Oh yes. They're at work.' I said, 'You're not wearing them for work. They're good slacks are them.' He said, 'They're shit-coloured. What do I want with shit-coloured trousers?'

He was in the yard swilling his boots when he was saying all this. Outside. He's started being much more careful about all that. I don't know what's got into him

Fade

Lad opposite just delivering four pizzas to No. 17. She's a widow, living on her own with a son in New Zealand and a heart condition, what's she wanting with four pizzas? I bet she's never had a pizza in her life. They must think I'm stupid. The doctor said, 'Why can't you sleep?' I said, 'The police are bugging my home.' She said, 'Yes. There's a lot of it about.' Asian too. They're normally a bit more civil.

We went out in the van the other night and he stopped it somewhere and said, 'Do you think it's me?' I said, 'No.' He said, 'Well, my mam does. It was her that went to the police.' 'And what did they say?' 'Told her she wasn't the only one. Mothers queuing up apparently.' I said, 'Well, she might cut a bit more ice if she didn't wear that leopard-skin coat thing. Legacy from when she was at it herself.' 'At what?' 'Soliciting.' He said, 'Who told you that?' I said, 'You did. You said she was hard up.' He said, 'It was years ago. I was still at school.'

Went out with Tina later on and comes in all worked up again. Sets to. Thought he was going to go through the bed. And saying stuff out loud again. I thought of them across the road, listening, so I put my hand over his mouth at one point, which he seemed to like.

I waited to see if there was anything in the papers only there wasn't. Been nothing for about a week now. You can get things out of proportion, I think.

I found where they'd put their listening thing this morning. Little hole in the skirting board. Did it when he was reckoning to go to the lavatory. Must have been quick because he'd managed to colour it white so it didn't show only some fluff got stuck to the paint so that's how I spotted it.

Sound of a newspaper coming through the door. She picks it up.

They've found another one, it looks like. This time on a skip. Been there... about a week.

Fade

One of them leaps over the wall, quite unnecessarily in my opinion because the gate's wide open. They get it off the TV. Five police cars. Batter on the door and when he opens it bowl him over and put handcuffs on him and take him off with a jacket over his head.

Tina, of course is going mad and they've got a dog of their own which doesn't help. I said, 'You're not fetching that thing in here.' He said, 'We've got a warrant.' I said, 'His dog's not been in here so I don't see why your dog should.' He said, 'This is an instrument of law enforcement.' I said, 'Yes, and it's an instrument of urinating against lampposts and leaving parcels on pavements. I don't want it sniffing round my stuff.' He says, 'You've got no choice love,' and shoves me out of the way.

One of them's upstairs going through the airing cupboard. I said, 'What are you looking for? Maybe I can help?' He said, 'If you must know we're looking for the murder weapon.' I said, 'Oh, I can show you that. This is the murder weapon (*Points to her tongue*). This is always the murder weapon. You want to drag the canal for that.'

He said, 'You sound sicker than he does. I don't think you realise the seriousness of your situation. If we find you know what's been going on you'll be in the dock yourself.' I said, 'Don't put those sheets back. I shall have them all to wash now you've been handling them.' He said, 'We shall want all his clothes and other selected items,' and produces a roll of bin bags. 'Is everything here? He hasn't got anything at the dry cleaners?' I said, 'No.' I said, 'How do I know we'll get all this stuff back?' He said, 'That's the least of your worries.'

When eventually they go the handler reckons to take charge of Tina, except that he can't get her to go in the car with them. Then when they do force her in they all pile out sharpish because she's straightaway done her business in the car. I laughed.

It was suddenly quiet when they'd gone, just Mother Catchpole at her gate shouting. 'The doctor says I'm clinically depressed. That dog wants putting down.'

The police said not to touch anything but I wasn't having the place left upset like that so I set to and cleaned down and repaired the ravages a bit. One or two folks outside the house looking in and the phone rings now and again but I don't answer.

Dark by the time I'd finished but I didn't turn the lights on, just sat there. They must have charged him around six because suddenly there's cars drawing up and the phone's going like mad and reporters banging on the door and shouting through the letter-box and whatnot.

I just sit there in the dark and don't take on.

Fade

Another parcel of excrement through the letter-box this morning. Postmarked Selby. Pleasant place. We had a little run there once in the van. Saw the cathedral, abbey, whatever it is. Shop with booklets and teatowels the way they do. Had a cup of coffee at a café down a street. The postman whanged it through that hard it split on the doormat.

It's probably deliberate. I'd got some plastic down from the previous times but still I'd to set to again. Spend a fortune on Dettol.

The trial's in Manchester for some reason. Out of the area. They can't call me unless I choose. Which I don't. Woman spat at me in Sainsbury's so I shop at the Asian shops now. Everywhere else they stare. Have to go thirty miles to get a perm. Go by minicab. Asians again. Never liked them much before. Don't ask questions. Godsend.

Reporter comes ringing the doorbell this afternoon. I think they must take it in turns. Shouts through the letter-box. I said, 'You want to be careful with that letter-box. You don't know what's been through it.' Says I'm sitting on a gold mine. Talks about £10,000. My side of the story.

Final speeches today. It rests on the dog, apparently, the rest is circumstantial. The van seen where the murders were, stopped once even but nothing else. Nothing on his tools. Nothing on his clothes. Only they found some blood belonging to the last one on the dog. The defence says it could have rolled in the blood because with the dog being fastened up all day when they went off he let it roam all over. So it doesn't mean he was with her, or anywhere near as the dog was off the lead.

The judge likes dogs. Has a dog of his own apparently. I don't know that'll make any difference.

I saw him before the trial started. Looked thinner. I was disappointed not to see him wearing a tie. I thought a tie would have made a good impression only they use them to commit suicide apparently.

I wish I'd something to do. I've cleaned down twice already. The yard wants doing only I can't do it with folks and reporters hanging about.

Pause

He's lying, of course. Our Tina hasn't been seen to, so when he takes her out he never lets her off the lead. Ever.

Fade

'Marjory! Marjory!'
    They still shout over the gate now and again, one of them there this morning. Most of them have gone only they leave a couple of young ones here just in case I go shopping. Jury's been out two days now and they think it might be a week.
    Anyway I thought while the heat was off I might be able to sneak out into the yard and give the kennel a good going over. The forensics took away her blanket so that's a blessing. I said to the feller, 'Don't bother to fetch it back. I'd have wuthered it long since if he'd let me.'
    I peeped out of the gate to see if it's safe to swill and there's just a couple of the young reporters sat on Mrs C's doorstep having a cup of tea. I don't know what she's going to do when it's all over. She's had the time of her life.
    Anyway I chucked a bucket of water under the kennel and then another only it didn't seem to be coming out the other side. I thought it was muck that had built up or something so I went in and got a wire coat hanger and started scraping about underneath and there's something there.
    It was his tan slacks, all mucky and plastered up with something. I sneaked in and got a bin bag and fetched them inside.
    Thinking back the police had been round with the dog but I suppose it couldn't smell anything except Tina. I sit there staring at this bag wondering whether there's anybody I should ring up. Suddenly there's a banging at the door and a voice through the letter-box.
    'Marjory! Marjory!'
    I didn't listen I ran with the bag and put it in the cupboard under the stairs. More clattering at the door.
    'Marjory! Marjory! They've come back, the jury. He's been acquitted. He's got off. Can we have a picture?'

Fade

The young woman says, 'Did I want any assistance with costume or styling? There'll be a lot of photographers.' I said, 'What's the matter with what I've got on?' She said, 'I could arrange for someone to come round and give you a shampoo and set.' I said, 'Yes, I could arrange for someone to come round and give you a kick up the arse.'

Though come to think of it I couldn't actually. She said, 'The paper's got a lot of money invested in you.' I said, 'Well, that's your funeral.'

Picture of him and the dog on the front page this morning, dog licking his face, ears up, paws on his shoulder, loving every minute of it. Spent the night in a hotel, five star, paid for by the newspaper. Article 'These nightmare months.' I stood by him, apparently. Says the longed-for reunion with his wife Marjory is scheduled for sometime this afternoon.

Police furious. The inspector in charge of the investigation said, 'Put it this way. We are not looking for anybody else.'

Sat waiting all afternoon. Photographers standing on the wall opposite, and on chairs and kitchen stools, two of them on top of a car. One up a tree. Police keeping the crowds back.

Getting dark when a big car draws up. Pandemonium.

Policeman bangs on the door, and Stuart's stood there on the doorstep and all the cameras going and them shouting, 'Stuart, Marjory. Over here. Over here please.' They want pictures of us with the dog, only the fellow from the newspaper says, No. They're going to be exclusive, apparently.

I said, 'Well, I've washed her kennel.' He says, 'She's not staying in there.' I said, 'You're not fetching her inside.' He said, 'I bloody am.' I said, 'Well, she'll have to stay on her paper.'

Later on when we're going to bed I wanted to shut her downstairs in the kitchen but he wouldn't have that either, keeps kissing her and whatnot and says she has to come upstairs.

When we're in bed he starts on straightaway and keeps asking Tina if she's taking it all in.

Afterwards he said, 'Are you surprised I'm not guilty?' I said, 'I'm surprised you got off.' He said, 'Don't you think I'm not guilty?' I said, 'I don't know, do I?' He said, 'You bloody do. You'd better bloody know. You're as bad as my mam.' I said, 'I'm not your mam.' He said, 'No, you're bloody not' and laughs.

I must have fallen asleep because when I wake up he's sleeping and the dog's off its paper, sat on his side of the bed watching him.

I get up and go downstairs and get the bin bag from under the stairs only I don't put any lights on. Then I get the poker and go out into the yard and push the slacks back under the kennel.

It's a bit moonlight and when I look over the gate they've all gone, just a broken chair on the pavement opposite.

I get back into bed and in a bit he wakes up and he has another go.

Fade

Comparing the texts

Now that you have read all four texts in this chapter, think about the following comparisons and contrasts between them.

- How successful are the different authors in making you sympathise with the central character in each text?
- Which of these texts is most successful at conveying a sense of guilt, and why?
- How do the different genre qualities of ballad, short story and television script influence the **content** and structure of each text?
- What effect does the social and historical setting of each text have on its content and on the ideas or attitudes it conveys?
- What can you learn from these texts about some of the ways in which the English language has changed in the last two centuries?

Writing about the texts

When you have reached some conclusions about these issues, or any others which come to your mind, consider a written response to *one* of the following tasks.

Tasks

4   In *Mr Policeman and the Cook* the policeman tries to excuse himself for neglecting his duty, while in *The Outside Dog* Marjory suggests she has no control over the situation. Which author is more successful at gaining your sympathy for the main character's failings, and why?

5   Both *A Trampwoman's Tragedy* and *A Confession Found in a Prison in the Time of Charles the Second* are set in historical periods before the time in which they were written. How have the authors used these settings to add to the effect of the texts, and which is the more successful in your opinion?

6   For this task use **either** *A Trampwoman's Tragedy* and *Mr Policeman and the Cook* **or** *A Confession Found in a Prison in the Time of Charles the Second* and *The Outside Dog*. Both texts involve a character who commits murder, but who is not necessarily the main character. How does each author make you understand the murderer's motives? Do you feel more sympathy for one than the other, and why?

7   All four of these texts are written in the first person. How does each author use this technique to involve you in situations and to encourage you to form your own opinions about the main characters? Which of the four authors is the most successful at this, and why?

Glossaries

Thomas Hardy, *A Trampwoman's Tragedy*

afoot	on foot
declined	in the sky
dropt	gave birth to
ere	before
figured	were visible
fosseway	ancient track
gilded	made golden in colour
glazing	staring
idleness	boredom
landskip	landscape
lea	field or meadow
like	likely
livelong	whole
lone	lonely
nigh	close to
realm	kingdom
renowned	well-known
settle	high-backed seat
slant	sloping
stray	wander
tap	pub or inn
tending	looking after, caring for
thereaft	afterwards
thinned	disappeared
toilsome	difficult
tor	hill
turnpike	toll
wanton	cruel
wild	countryside
won	reached
wooed	sought affection or love

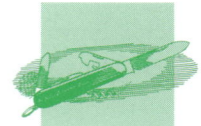

Wilkie Collins, *Mr Policeman and the Cook*

abstain	do not
answered for	guaranteed
append	attach
area	basement
citing	naming
concluded	decided
constitutionally	physically
Creole	from the West Indies
cutlers	manufacturers of knives
demented	mad, deranged
diminution	reduction

dissipated	wasted, immoral
distracted	mad
embarkation	sailing
engaged	busy, occupied
fatality	something caused by fate
form	procedure
gallows	scaffold (for hanging someone)
garret	attic room
girdle	belt
goat's	goatee
grog	rum diluted with water
harassed	bothered, worried
implements	tools
insensibility	insensitivity
larceny	theft
like	similar
make love	declare a liking
own	admit
partial to	admired
pattern	model, ideal
pecuniary	financial
penance	confession
perpendicularly	upright
perpetually	continuously
perversity	trick
pluck	courage
portmanteau	large travelling case or trunk
prodigious	amazing
profligate	extravagant
prostrated	exhausted
recognizance	agreement
station	social class
station-house	police station
strung	strengthened
subsistence	existence
well-nigh	almost
yielded	gave in

Charles Dickens, *A Confession Found in a Prison in the Time of Charles the Second*

absorbing	most important
abstaining	not doing
accomplished	talented
ague	fever
ardently	passionately
astir	blowing
avowal	statement

bade	told
bauble	toy
brink	edge
careering	racing, running
commission	rank
compassing	plotting
concluded	agreed
confided	gave
diminished	reduced
divest	rid
doom	fate
earnestly	seriously, with concentration
endeavouring	attempting
expedite	hurry
faculties	mind
fancy	imagination
foreshadowing	premonition
fraught	filled
gall	bitterness
hard	close
in right of	through marriage to
instrumental	the means by which
interposition	intervention
lighted	landed
lisp	speak
marked	noticed
meditated	intended
prattling	talking excitedly
rankling	bitter
resolved	decided
scouts	searchers
serviceable	useful
snuff	sniff, smell
steal	creep
stole	crept
supplication	prayer
supplied	taken
thicket	dense growth of small trees or shrubs
tremendous	terrible

Alan Bennett, *The Outside Dog*

appliance	surgical fitting
bugging	fitting listening devices
circumstantial	indirect, inconclusive
cultivated	reasonable, sensible
cut…ice	get listened to
dolled	made

evolution	development of species
fly-tipping	illegally dumping rubbish
forensics	police who look for medical evidence
jimmy riddle	urinate
legacy	something left over
lolling	hanging
muff	noise
pandemonium	noisy, chaotic
province	business, interest
ravages	damage
shop	place
signatory	someone who signs a document
sizing…up	having a good look round
slacks	casual trousers
swill	clean
whanged	threw
wuthered	thrown away

Staying or going: diverse texts

Introduction

This chapter contains extracts from two texts which at first might seem so different that no comparison between them could be possible or useful. One is from a nineteenth-century novel, the other from a recent radio play. One is about a teenage girl about to embark on adult life, the other about a seven-year-old girl who is terminally ill. One is written in the third person, with description and dialogue, the other is a first-person monologue.

So much for the contrasts. But as you read each extract, think about less obvious connections: the fears and certainties expressed by both Eppie and Spoonface; the concerns and motives of the adults whose lives they both touch on.

Reading the George Eliot

The first extract is from *Silas Marner* by George Eliot, a masculine name adopted by Marian (or Mary Ann) Evans in an age when women writers were not treated as seriously as their male counterparts. This novel, quite short by Victorian standards, was published in 1861. It tells the story of Silas Marner, a linen-weaver in the Midlands, who suffered unfair treatment in his earlier life and has now become a lonely man obsessed with the growing pile of gold he earns from his trade. This gold is stolen, but soon afterwards a young child, Eppie, mysteriously turns up on his doorstep. Silas adopts her, and she gives him a new purpose in life.

Sixteen years later, a chance discovery means that Silas' gold is returned to him and the local landowner, Godfrey Cass, now married to Nancy, admits to being Eppie's father by a previous secret marriage. Eppie's mother was a working-class woman who died near Silas' cottage on the night that Eppie was found. In this extract, Godfrey and Nancy visit Silas and Eppie with a proposal concerning Eppie's future.

As you read it, think about the following issues.

- How does George Eliot convey the strength of feeling between Silas and Eppie?
- How does the author use her role as storyteller to influence your reactions to what happens?
- Why do Godfrey and Nancy assume that Eppie will want to go and live with them?
- How do the different characters seem realistic through the language they use and the attitudes they display?
- Does George Eliot want you to feel any sympathy for Godfrey and Nancy? Why?

From Silas Marner *by George Eliot*

Claiming Eppie

BETWEEN EIGHT and nine o'clock that evening, Eppie and Silas were seated alone in the cottage. After the great excitement the weaver had undergone from the events of the afternoon, he had felt a longing for this quietude, and had even begged Mrs Winthrop and Aaron, who had naturally lingered behind every one else, to leave him alone with his child. The excitement had not passed away; it had only reached that stage when the keenness of the susceptibility makes external stimulus intolerable – when there is no sense of weariness, but rather an intensity of inward life under which sleep is an impossibility. Any one who has watched such moments in other men remembers the brightness of the eyes and the strange definiteness that comes over coarse features from that transient influence. It is as if a new fineness of ear for all spiritual voices had sent wonder-working vibrations through the heavy mortal frame – as if "beauty born of murmuring sound" had passed into the face of the listener.

Silas's face showed that sort of transfiguration as he sat in his arm-chair and looked at Eppie. She had drawn her own chair towards his knees, and leaned forward, holding both his hands, while she looked up at him. On the table near them, lit by a candle, lay the recovered gold – the old long-loved gold, ranged in orderly heaps, as Silas used to range it in the days when it was his only joy. He had been telling her how he used to count it every night, and how his soul was utterly desolate till she was sent to him.

"At first I'd a sort o' feeling come across me now and then," he was saying in a subdued tone, "as if you might be changed into the gold again; for sometimes, turn my head which way I would, I seemed to see the gold; and I thought I should be glad if I could feel it, and find it was come back. But that didn't last long. After a bit I should have thought it was a curse come again if it had drove you from me, for I'd got to feel the need o' your looks and your voice and the touch o' your little fingers. You didn't know then, Eppie, when you were such a little un – you didn't know what your old father Silas felt for you."

"But I know now, father," said Eppie. "If it hadn't been for you, they'd have taken me to the workhouse, and there'd have been nobody to love me."

"Eh, my precious child, the blessing was mine. If you hadn't been sent to save me, I should ha' gone to the grave in my misery. The money was taken from me in time; and you see it's been kept – kept till it was wanted for you. It's wonderful – our life is wonderful."

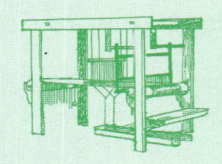

Silas sat in silence a few minutes, looking at the money. "It takes no hold of me now," he said, ponderingly – "the money doesn't. I wonder if it ever could again – I doubt it might if I lost you, Eppie. I might come to think I was forsaken again, and lose the feeling that God was good to me."

At that moment there was a knocking at the door; and Eppie was obliged to rise without answering Silas. Beautiful she looked, with the tenderness of gathering tears in her eyes and a slight flush on her cheeks as she stepped to open the door. The flush deepened when she saw Mr and Mrs Godfrey Cass. She made her little rustic curtsy and held the door wide for them to enter.

"We're disturbing you very late, my dear," said Mrs Cass, taking Eppie's hand, and looking in her face with an expression of anxious interest and admiration. Nancy herself was pale and tremulous. Eppie, after placing chairs for Mr and Mrs Cass, went to stand against Silas, opposite to them.

"Well, Marner," said Godfrey, trying to speak with perfect firmness, "it's a great comfort to me to see you with your money again, that you've been deprived of so many years. It was one of my family did you the wrong – the more grief to me and I feel bound to make up to you for it in every way. Whatever I can do for you will be nothing but paying a debt, even if I looked no further than the robbery. But there are other things I'm beholden – shall be beholden to you for, Marner."

Godfrey checked himself. It had been agreed between him and his wife that the subject of his fatherhood should be approached very carefully, and that, if possible, the disclosure should be reserved for the future, so that it might be made to Eppie gradually. Nancy had urged this, because she felt strongly the painful light in which Eppie must inevitably see the relation between her father and mother.

Silas, always ill at ease when he was being spoken to by "betters", such as Mr Cass – tall, powerful, florid men, seen chiefly on horseback – answered with some constraint, –

"Sir, I've a deal to thank you for a'ready. As for the robbery, I count it no loss to me. And if I did, you couldn't help it; you aren't answerable for it."

"You may look at it in that way, Marner, but I never can; and I hope you'll let me act according to my own feeling of what's just. I know you're easily contented; you've been a hard-working man all your life."

"Yes, sir, yes," said Marner, meditatively. "I should ha' been bad off without my work; it was what I held by when everything else was gone from me."

"Ah," said Godfrey, applying Marner's words simply to his bodily wants, "it was a good trade for you in this country, because there's been a great deal of linen-weaving to be done. But you're getting rather past such close work, Marner; it's time you laid by and had some rest. You look a good deal pulled down, though you're not an old man, *are* you?"

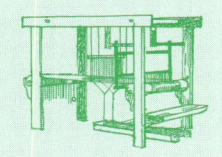

"Fifty-five, as near as I can say, sir," said Silas.

"Oh, why, you may live thirty years longer – look at old Macey! And that money on the table, after all, is but little. It won't go far either way – whether it's put out to interest, or you were to live on it as long as it would last; it wouldn't go far if you'd nobody to keep but yourself, and you've had two to keep for a good many years now."

"Eh, sir," said Silas, unaffected by anything Godfrey was saying, "I am in no fear o' want. We shall do very well – Eppie and me 'ull do well enough. There's few working-folks have got so much laid by as that. I don't know what it is to gentlefolks, but I look upon it as a deal – almost too much. And as for us, it's little we want."

"Only the garden, father," said Eppie, blushing up to the ears the moment after.

"You love a garden, do you, my dear?" said Nancy, thinking that this turn in the point of view might help her husband. "We should agree in that; I give a deal of time to the garden."

"Ah, there's plenty of gardening at the Red House," said Godfrey, surprised at the difficulty he found in approaching a proposition which had seemed so easy to him in the distance. "You've done a good part by Eppie, Marner, for sixteen years. It 'ud be a great comfort to you to see her well provided for, wouldn't it? She looks blooming and healthy, but not fit for any hardships; she doesn't look like a strapping girl come of working parents. You'd like to see her taken care of by those who can leave her well off, and make a lady of her; she's more fit for it than for a rough life, such as she might come to have in a few years' time."

A slight flush came over Marner's face, and disappeared, like a passing gleam. Eppie was simply wondering Mr Cass should talk so about things that seemed to have nothing to do with reality; but Silas was hurt and uneasy.

"I don't take your meaning, sir," he answered, not having words at command to express the mingled feelings with which he had heard Mr Cass's words.

"Well, my meaning is this, Marner," said Godfrey, determined to come to the point. "Mrs Cass and I, you know, have no children – nobody to be the better for our good home and everything else we have – more than enough for ourselves. And we should like to have somebody in the place of a daughter to us – we should like to have Eppie, and treat her in every way as our own child. It would be a great comfort to you in your old age, I hope, to see her fortune made in that way, after you've been at the trouble of bringing her up so well. And it's right you should have every reward for that. And Eppie, I'm sure, will always love you and be grateful to you; she'd come and see you very often, and we should all be on the look-out to do everything we could towards making you comfortable."

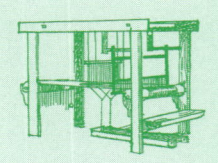

A plain man like Godfrey Cass, speaking under some embarrassment, necessarily blunders on words that are coarser than his intentions, and that are likely to fall gratingly on susceptible feelings. While he had been speaking, Eppie had quietly passed her arm behind Silas's head, and let her hand rest against it caressingly: she felt him trembling violently. He was silent for some moments when Mr Cass had ended – powerless under the conflict of emotions, all alike painful. Eppie's heart was swelling at the sense that her father was in distress; and she was just going to lean down and speak to him, when one struggling dread at last gained the mastery over every other in Silas, and he said, faintly:

"Eppie, my child, speak. I won't stand in your way. Thank Mr and Mrs Cass."

Eppie took her hand from her father's head, and came forward a step. Her cheeks were flushed, but not with shyness this time: the sense that her father was in doubt and suffering banished that sort of self-consciousness. She dropt a low curtsy, first to Mrs Cass and then to Mr Cass, and said:

"Thank you, ma'am – thank you, sir. But I can't leave my father, nor own anybody nearer than him. And I don't want to be a lady – thank you all the same" (here Eppie dropped another curtsy). "I couldn't give up the folks I've been used to."

Eppie's lip began to tremble a little at the last words. She retreated to her father's chair again, and held him round the neck: while Silas, with a subdued sob, put up his hand to grasp hers.

The tears were in Nancy's eyes, but her sympathy with Eppie was naturally divided with distress on her husband's account. She dared not speak, wondering what was going on in her husband's mind.

Godfrey felt an irritation inevitable to almost all of us when we encounter an unexpected obstacle. He had been full of his own penitence and resolution to retrieve his error as far as the time was left to him; he was possessed with all-important feelings, that were to lead to a pre-determined course of action which he had fixed on as the right, and he was not prepared to enter with lively appreciation into other people's feelings counteracting his virtuous resolves. The agitation with which he spoke again was not quite unmixed with anger.

"But I've a claim on you, Eppie – the strongest of all claims. It's my duty, Marner, to own Eppie as my child, and provide for her. She is my own child – her mother was my wife. I have a natural claim on her that must stand before every other."

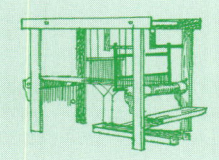

Eppie had given a violent start, and turned quite pale. Silas, on the contrary, who had been relieved by Eppie's answer, from the dread lest his mind should be in opposition to hers, felt the spirit of resistance in him set free, not without a touch of parental fierceness. "Then, sir," he answered with an accent of bitterness that had been silent in him since the memorable day when his youthful hope had perished – "then, sir, why didn't you say so sixteen year ago, and claim her before I'd come to love her, i'stead o' coming to take her from me now, when you might as well take the heart out o' my body? God gave her to me because you turned your back upon her, and He looks upon her as mine. You've no right to her! When a man turns a blessing from his door, it falls to them as take it in."

"I know that, Marner. I was wrong. I've repented of my conduct in that matter," said Godfrey, who could not help feeling the edge of Silas's words.

"I am glad to hear it, sir," said Marner with gathering excitement; "but repentance doesn't alter what's been going on for sixteen year. Your coming now and saying 'I'm her father', doesn't alter the feelings inside us. It's me she's been calling her father ever since she could say the word."

"But I think you might look at the thing more reasonably, Marner," said Godfrey, unexpectedly awed by the weaver's direct truth-speaking. "It isn't as if she was to be taken quite away from you, so that you'd never see her again. She'll be very near you, and come to see you very often. She'll feel just the same towards you."

"Just the same?" said Marner, more bitterly than ever. "How'll she feel just the same for me as she does now, when we eat o' the same bit, and drink o' the same cup, and think o' the same things from one day's end to another? Just the same? That's idle talk. You'd cut us i' two."

Godfrey, unqualified by experience to discern the pregnancy of Marner's simple words, felt rather angry again. It seemed to him that the weaver was very selfish (a judgment readily passed by those who have never tested their own power of sacrifice) to oppose what was undoubtedly for Eppie's welfare; and he felt himself called upon, for her sake, to assert his authority.

"I should have thought, Marner," he said severely – "I should have thought affection for Eppie would have made you rejoice in what was for her good, even if it did call upon you to give up something. You ought to remember your own life is uncertain, and she's at an age now when her lot may soon be fixed in a way very different from what it would be in her father's home: she may marry some low working-man, and then, whatever I might do for her, I couldn't make her well-off. You're putting yourself in the way of her welfare; and though I'm sorry to hurt you after what you've done, and what I've left undone, I feel now it's my duty to insist on taking care of my own daughter. I want to do my duty."

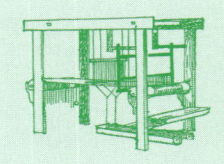

It would be difficult to say whether it were Silas or Eppie that was most deeply stirred by this last speech of Godfrey's. Thought had been very busy in Eppie as she listened to the contest between her old, long-loved father and this new unfamiliar father who had suddenly come to fill the place of that black featureless shadow which had held the ring and placed it on her mother's finger. Her imagination had darted backward in conjectures, and forward in previsions, of what this revealed fatherhood implied; and there were words in Godfrey's last speech which helped to make the previsions especially definite. Not that these thoughts, either of past or future, determined her resolution – *that* was determined by the feelings which vibrated to every word Silas had uttered; but they raised, even apart from these feelings a repulsion towards the offered lot and the newly-revealed father.

Silas, on the other hand, was again stricken in conscience, and alarmed lest Godfrey's accusation should be true – lest he should be raising his own will as an obstacle to Eppie's good. For many moments he was mute, struggling for the self-conquest necessary to the uttering of the difficult words. They came out tremulously.

"I'll say no more. Let it be as you will. Speak to the child. I'll hinder nothing."

Even Nancy, with all the acute sensibility of her own affections, shared her husband's view, that Marner was not justifiable in his wish to retain Eppie, after her real father had avowed himself. She felt that it was a very hard trial for the poor weaver, but her code allowed no question that a father by blood must have a claim above that of any foster-father. Besides, Nancy, used all her life to plenteous circumstances and the privileges of "respectability", could not enter into the pleasures which early nurture and habit connect with all the little aims and efforts of the poor who are born poor: to her mind, Eppie, in being restored to her birthright, was entering on a too long withheld but unquestionable good. Hence she heard Silas's last words with relief, and thought, as Godfrey did, that their wish was achieved.

"Eppie, my dear," said Godfrey – looking at his daughter, not without some embarrassment under the sense that she was old enough to judge him – "it'll always be our wish that you should show your love and gratitude to one who's been a father to you so many years, and we shall want to help you to make him comfortable in every way. But we hope you'll come to love us as well; and though I haven't been what a father should have been to you all these years, I wish to do the utmost in my power for you for the rest of my life, and provide for you as my only child. And you'll have the best of mothers in my wife – that'll be a blessing you haven't known since you were old enough to know it."

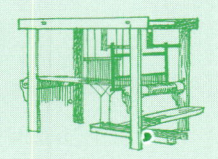

"My dear, you'll be a treasure to me," said Nancy, in her gentle voice. "We shall want for nothing when we have our daughter."

Eppie did not come forward and curtsy, as she had done before. She held Silas's hand in hers, and grasped it firmly – it was a weaver's hand, with a palm and finger-tips that were sensitive to such pressure – while she spoke with colder decision than before.

"Thank you, ma'am – thank you, sir, for your offers – they're very great, and far above my wish. For I should have no delight in life any more if I was forced to go away from my father, and knew he was sitting at home, a-thinking of me and feeling lone. We've been used to be happy together every day, and I can't think o' no happiness without him. And he says he'd nobody i' the world till I was sent to him, and he'd have nothing when I was gone. And he's took care of me and loved me from the first, and I'll cleave to him as long as he lives, and nobody shall ever come between him and me."

"But you must make sure, Eppie," said Silas, in a low voice – "you must make sure as you won't ever be sorry, because you've made your choice to stay among poor folks, and with poor clothes and things, when you might ha' had everything o' the best."

His sensitiveness on this point had increased as he listened to Eppie's words of faithful affection.

"I can never be sorry, father," said Eppie. "I shouldn't know what to think on or to wish for with fine things about me, as I haven't been used to. And it 'ud be poor work for me to put on things, and ride in a gig, and sit in a place at church, as 'ud make them as I'm fond of think me unfitting company for 'em. What could *I* care for then?"

Nancy looked at Godfrey with a pained questioning glance. But his eyes were fixed on the floor, where he was moving the end of his stick, as if he were pondering on something absently. She thought there was a word which might perhaps come better from her lips than from his.

"What you say is natural, my dear child; it's natural you should cling to those who've brought you up," she said, mildly; "but there's a duty you owe to your lawful father. There's perhaps something to be given up on more sides than one. When your father opens his home to you, I think it's right you shouldn't turn your back on it."

"I can't feel as I've got any father but one," said Eppie, impetuously, while the tears gathered. "I've always thought of a little home where he'd sit i' the corner, and I should fend and do everything for him. I can't think o' no other home.

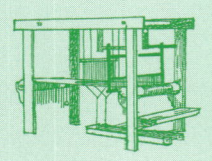

I wasn't brought up to be a lady, and I can't turn my mind to it. I like the working-folks, and their houses, and their ways. And," she ended passionately, while the tears fell, "I'm promised to marry a working-man, as'll live with father, and help me to take care of him."

Godfrey looked up at Nancy with a flushed face and smarting dilated eyes. This frustration of a purpose towards which he had set out under the exalted consciousness that he was about to compensate in some degree for the greatest demerit of his life, made him feel the air of the room stifling.

"Let us go," he said, in an undertone.

"We won't talk of this any longer now," said Nancy, rising. "We're your well-wishers, my dear – and yours too, Marner. We shall come and see you again. It's getting late now."

In this way she covered her husband's abrupt departure, for Godfrey had gone straight to the door, unable to say more.

Reading the Lee Hall

The second extract is from *Spoonface Steinberg*, a radio play by Lee Hall first broadcast in 1997 and later turned into a play for television. It has only one character, Spoonface herself. She is seven, and is near to death. In the final scene of the play she thinks about some of the people in her life, especially Mrs Spud the cleaner, and listens to opera music, which is her greatest love.

As you read the extract, think about the following issues.

- By writing in the form of a **radio script**, how has Lee Hall affected your response to the situation?
- Is Spoonface a convincing seven-year-old? What techniques does the author use to make you feel sympathetic towards her?
- How is the personality of Mrs Spud put across so strongly by the author, even though she is not an actual character in the play?
- After this play was first broadcast, the BBC was inundated with letters and calls from listeners who had been deeply affected by it. Why do you think it provoked such a reaction?

From Spoonface Steinberg by Lee Hall

MUSIC: *Maria Callas singing 'Vissi d'arte, vissi d'amore' from* Tosca *by Puccini*

During the day Mrs Spud comes in and sees me – she makes me stuff and that and helps out Mam with the laundry and the cleaning and she makes the house spick and span and that – if I was to grow up, I would be like Mrs Spud and everyday I would clean the fridge and the oven and the shelves and the steps out to the garden and some of the skirting boards, but I would leave the shelves where nobody looks and everything would be clean.

I asked Mrs Spud where I got my cancer from and she did not know – I said, I think I might have caught it off God and she said God does not have cancer as far as we know – I said, maybe he's just not telling anybody – Mrs Spud says that if God has got cancer we're all in trouble – I think maybe he has or he has not.

She said she has a son who is a little angel and a husband who is dead – he had the cancer too – only his was of a difference – she did weep when she told me about him and how when they were just children they met and he kissed her on the neck and that – and on those days that the sun shone forever – she said that the trouble is when people are around – you forget that they are quite special and when they are gone it is too late to tell them and you must always tell them – she said there was nobody like her husband and that he was a very kind man to her – and when she spoke of him you could tell as her eyes were sparkly and her breath was warm – and although he was gone away he was also here – and that every day they had a little chat – and how was the weather and in heaven it never rained – she said we would all be there in the same place one day and maybe I'll get to meet him – I said I didn't know if I could go to there on account of being Jewish – but she was sure I would – his name was Mr Spud.

Then I said that I quite liked the rain when it was wet and it blew so grey on the ground and I would watch from the bed when the trees would weep and bend in the day – and I saw how the shed wobbled in the wind – and I would see the cloud for all the silver there was in it – and every day of the rain, the sun even in its little bits made the world spark like diamonds and glisten in the weather – and if I was in heaven there would be no dull to shine out in the sad days – but Mrs Spud said she liked the sun and when she could afford she would go on a nice holiday in Ibiza – although Jimmy – which is her son – would not go on account of the price – which is a shame.

I asked her if she was lonely without poor Mr Spud – she said a bit and that she would lie and remember him whenever – but then again we are not gone – then I said, did she see that there was blackness and she did not – she said there was sadness and stuff but that's what there is – but if you look there is also happiness – like little children having a smile – or someone with a birthday – and even in a graveyard there might be a little butterfly flying round the gravestones – and these are the things what is important – and poor Mr Spud would be sad in heaven if he thought that Mrs Spud didn't look at the day and see that in the trees and in the sky there was a little piece of heaven.

I felt sad for Mrs Spud as she had three hungry mouths to feed – her and Jimmy and someone else – and one day she came into my room to do the hoovering and I had poo'd in my pants and it was a disgusting smell and she cleaned my bum and the bed for me – and I made her a card the next day – and it said 'I love You Mrs Spud' – and she cried – and she cried when she got it – she said, what a lovely card – and I said I did my best considering the crayons I had which was not very many and there was no blue so there was no proper sky – but she said it was quite a beautiful card for a cleaner.

MUSIC: *Maria Callas singing 'Vissi d'arte, vissi d'amore' from* Tosca

When you think about dying it is very hard to do – it is to think about what is not – to think about everything there is nothing – to not be and never to be again – it is even more than emptiness – if you think of emptiness it is full of nothing and death is more than this – death is even less than nothing – when you think about that you will not be here for your breakfast – and that you will never see Mam or Dad or Mrs Spud – or the telly or hear the sweet singing opera ladies or feel anything any more – but you won't feel sad as there will be nothing to feel of – and that is the weird point – not that there is even anything but there is not even nothing – and that is death.

Sometimes it is scary – but to think that I'll not be is impossible because I'm here – and when I'm not here there'll still be cows and grass and vegetables and radios and telephone machines and cardiologists and soup tins and cookers and hats and shoes and Walkmans and Tiny Tears and synagogues and beaches and sunshine and walks in the rain and films and music and my coat and my shoes and cars and underpants and necklaces and my Mam and Dad and flowers – everywhere there'll be something in the whole world everything will be full except me – and there isn't even a hole somewhere where I used to be – and apart from people what remember me and what I was like there is nothing missing from when I was here – there is no space in the universe where people have dropped out – it is all filled in as full as ever – there is nothing to know, as is everything that there is, is all around us – there is nothing to know because there it is – in the world everything is divided – everything divided one from the other one, from the many – from the mother and from the father – there is day and night and black and white and all these things but in the very beginning and in the end – everything will not be divided and there will be no me or you – there will be no this or that, no little puppy dogs or anything, there will only be that everything is the same – and every moment is forever – and it will shine and it will be everything and nothing – and that is all there is to know – that all of us will end up being one – and that is nothing – and it is endless.

MUSIC: *Maria Callas singing 'Ebben? ne andrò lontana' from* La Wally *by Catalani*

Blessed and lauded, glorified and lifted and exalted and enhanced and elevated and praised be the Name of the Holy One,
Blessed be he although he is high above all blessings, hymns and uplifts that can be voices in this world.
May his name be blessed for ever and ever. *(The Kaddish)*

THE END

Comparing the texts

Now that you have read both extracts, think about the following points of contrast and comparison.

- Do you feel sympathy for both Eppie and Spoonface, or not? What aspects of the writers' techniques and attitudes to their characters make you react in this way?
- Do either – or both – of these texts present a **sentimental** view of their main characters? Why (not)?
- What are the differences in the language used by George Eliot and Lee Hall, and how important are they in influencing your response to the texts?
- How do the different cultures and times in which these extracts are set affect your response to them?
- What do you think is the main theme or idea each author is trying to convey in these extracts? Is either – or both – of them an **optimistic** or a **pessimistic** text?

Writing about the texts

When you have discussed these and other issues, decide whether you could plan a successful response to *one* of the following tasks.

Tasks

8 The extracts from *Silas Marner* and *Spoonface Steinberg* both describe situations which are highly emotional. How successfully does each writer convey this depth of feeling to you? How does each use the qualities of the chosen genre (i.e. novel and radio script) to affect your response?

9 How does each author use Godfrey and Nancy in *Silas Marner* and Mrs Spud in *Spoonface Steinberg* to add to your understanding of Eppie's and Spoonface's feelings about their situation?

10 Describe how these extracts highlight differences in social and cultural attitudes between the times in which they are set. Explain how the writers use some of these attitudes to present their ideas and to affect your response to the situations and characters.

Glossaries

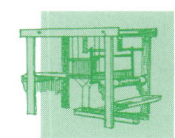

George Eliot, Silas Marner

a deal	a lot
acute	sharp
alike	similarly
avowed	revealed
(be) beholden (to)	to owe to
cleave	hold on
close	fine, detailed
code	way of life
conjectures	guesses
constraint	reserve
counteracting	going against
demerit	misconduct
desolate	empty, miserable
determined	decided
dilated	enlarged
discern	understand
disclosure	revelation
exalted	raised
fend	support
florid	red-complexioned
forsaken	abandoned
gig	two-wheeled, horse-drawn carriage
impetuously	rashly, hastily
lest	that
lot	fate, future
nurture	upbringing
penitence	shame
plenteous	rich

ponderingly	thoughtfully
pregnancy	full meaning
previsions	ideas about the future
proposition	suggestion
quietude	peace
range(d)	arrange(d)
resolution	decision
rustic	plain
sensibility	awareness
start	movement, slight jump
susceptibility	being overcome by emotion
transfiguration	enormous change
transient	passing
tremulous	nervous
want for	lack
workhouse	home for people unable to support themselves

Lee Hall, Spoonface Steinberg

cardiologist	doctors specialising in heart diseases
Ebben? Ne andrò lontana	Well then, shall I go far away from them?
elevated	raised up
enhanced	made greater
exalted	glorified
Ibiza	island holiday resort in Spain
Kaddish	a Jewish prayer that glorifies God for all things
lauded	praised
synagogue	building where Jewish religious services are held
Tiny Tears	a doll which makes crying noises
uplifts	improves spiritually
Vissi d'arte, vissi d'amore	I have lived for art, I have lived for love
Walkman	personal cassette player

Death or glory: texts on a theme

Introduction

The five texts in this chapter describe experiences and situations related to war. The wars concerned span more than two hundred years and involve different nations and societies: the two World Wars of this century, the American Civil War in the mid 1800s and the Napoleonic Wars between France and England at the start of the last century.

As in Chapters 2 and 3, there is a mix of genres so that you can compare the effect of genre features, as well as the content and setting of the texts. There are two extracts from full-length novels, one twentieth-century and one nineteenth-century; a complete nineteenth-century short story; and two poems from the early twentieth century, one of which is a short **lyric** and the other a longer **narrative**/descriptive poem.

Many well-known texts on the subject of war describe graphically the horrors of the fighting itself. This selection is different; although injury, maiming and death are never far away – and indeed are central issues in some of the texts – the settings are more domestic, the concerns personal rather than political or military. When you have read and considered these texts, you may find it interesting to compare the effects they have on you with those achieved by well-known poems by Wilfred Owen or Siegfried Sassoon, for example. If the comparison is helpful, you might consider using your wider reading around this theme as the starting-point for Task 20 in Chapter 5, page 129.

Reading the H.E. Bates

The opening extract comes from a novel about the Second World War, *Fair Stood the Wind for France* by H.E. Bates. This was published in 1944 while the War was still in progress, and part of the author's purpose was undoubtedly to raise national morale and to persuade the British public that their cause was worth fighting for and winning. Despite this, it is not just a piece of **propaganda**, as the focus is very much on the personal story of John Franklin, the pilot of a plane which crash-lands in Occupied France. He badly injures his arm, and is nursed to health by the family of a French farmer; he falls in love with Françoise, the daughter, and this extract begins when Franklin regains consciousness in the farmhouse after a local doctor has amputated part of his arm.

While you are reading it, think about:

- how the author conveys Franklin's confusion as he recovers from the effects of the anaesthetic, his changes of mood and how they are made real through the language
- the old woman's attitude towards Franklin and the war (she is Françoise's grandmother)
- why the author gives so little explicit detail about what has happened to Franklin's arm
- why the crucifix on the bedroom wall is mentioned twice
- what attitudes about war the author conveys through Franklin.

From
Fair Stood the Wind for France
by H. E. Bates

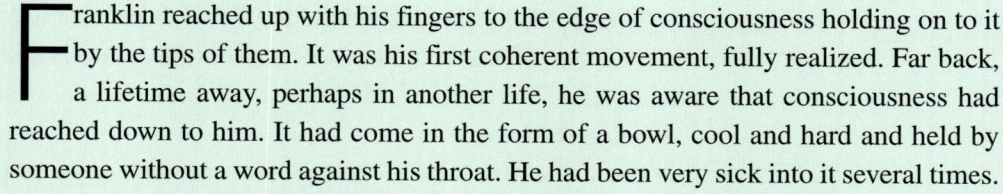

Franklin reached up with his fingers to the edge of consciousness holding on to it by the tips of them. It was his first coherent movement, fully realized. Far back, a lifetime away, perhaps in another life, he was aware that consciousness had reached down to him. It had come in the form of a bowl, cool and hard and held by someone without a word against his throat. He had been very sick into it several times.

His movement now was different. It was positive. He reached up with one hand, holding on to the ledge between darkness and light, waited for a moment before reaching up with the other. Then after a moment or two the horizon of light lowered and became steady. He was looking over the top.

The reality of everything was now heightened by the fact that everything was cut in half. He was lying flat on his back, so stiff that it seemed he might be strapped down, and he could see only the upper half of a chair, a chest of drawers, a window, the wounded upper half of the crucified Christ on the wall, and finally the upper half of the old woman, black and white and immobile, against the blue upper half of summer sky.

He pulled himself fully into consciousness and then became aware, at once, that he had never moved. He lay very still. To be still but also to be aware, to be aware but also to be alive, seemed suddenly miraculous.

He lay looking for some time at the sky. It was vastly blue and very distant. It fixed for him, for the first time, his sense of place. With such blueness, without cloud, he knew that he could never be in England. Through this realization, and through the clear hot blueness of the day, he finally became fully awake.

He became immediately aware of the tightness of his stomach. He needed the bed-bottle. In hospital, he understood, such desires were as natural as requests for tooth-brushes. Now he was faced with the necessity of translating it into another language. He lay thinking for some moments how the French were a people of good sense in fundamental things, but how also, in his French, there was no word for what he wanted to do. Then he knew, too, that it did not matter. He knew that nothing mattered: except perhaps the steadiness and beauty of the blue daylight beyond the window. As long as this light did not recede he knew that his life had been recaptured.

'Madame,' he said. He did not move as he spoke.

The old woman moved at once, as if she knew quite well he was conscious, and even as if she knew what he wanted.

'M'sieu,' she said. He watched her come fully, entire, over the edge of his vision. She stood by the bed with the sick-bowl in her hands.

'You want to be sick now? Again?' she said.

'No,' he said.

'You want something?'

'Yes.'

'What is it? You don't want to eat, do you?'

'No,' he said, 'I don't want to eat.' He searched his mind for the word, but could not find it. He knew one word, but it was, he felt, slightly lacking, even in French, in delicacy. He decided to try bottle.

'The bottle?' she said. Her face lifted itself slightly, unconcerned, earthy, too immensely old he thought to worry about the delicacy of life any longer. She moved away, and then, almost at once, came back. It appeared that the bottle had been standing ready.

The bottle was a dark claret bottle without a label and she came back with it on what was to him the left side of the bed. She held it out without concern. He did not even attempt to take it from her but lay with his right arm uplifted and dead still under the sheet, poised as his mind was poised in the oddest and most awful moment of his life. He was poised bodily as if he were going to overbalance and fall over sideways, like an aircraft without a wing. He knew in that moment that he had no left arm.

The old woman must have understood the moment. She stood quite still, holding the bottle but not speaking, waiting for the shock to pass. He did not move, partly through the shock but partly because of an absurd fear, acutely real, of falling out of bed.

'You will feel better when you have used it,' she said at last.

With some difficulty he raised his right arm above the coverlet. He still felt strapped down. He knew that the other arm was not there, but there was no sensation of emptiness, only of distrust. All of his body was stiff with caution. The fingers of his right hand outstretched themselves, stiffened and would move no further. The old woman was forced to put the bottle into it. He remembered then that he did not know what day it was, and wanted to ask her. 'Merci, madame. Merci beaucoup,' he said, but she had moved away.

She gave him two minutes, standing all the time by the window. He spent one of these minutes reaching over his right arm to the left side of himself. Where the left arm should have been there was a circular corset of bandage that wrapped over his chest; hence his feeling of being strapped down. It all seemed very clean and finished and neat. Feeling the shape of the bandage he thought, 'I have to know some time', and let his right hand slip down towards his waist. From somewhere about the height of his ribs there was nothing left. They had taken off the arm above the elbow.

'M'sieu has finished?'

She was standing by the bed. He smiled and drew the bottle out with ironic triumph, like a secret drinker. She smiled, too.

'What day is it?' he said. She took the bottle, meditatively. She might have been thinking, it seemed, that he had done very well. He felt it too.

'Wednesday,' she said. 'It was Monday when they operated.'

'Everything is all right?'

'With you? Yes,' she said.

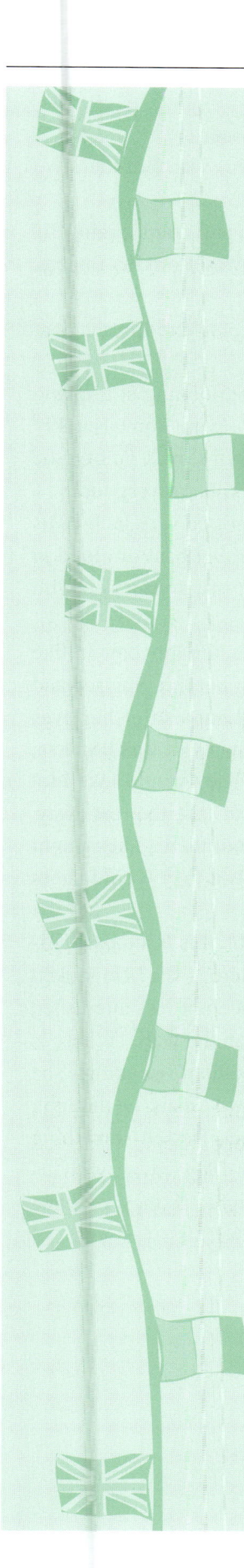

'No,' he said. 'Not only with me. But with the rest. With everything.'

She shrugged her shoulders and looked at the bottle. 'It is all right. If anything in France is all right.'

'I see,' he said.

'They say there have been riots up in the north. That will mean something.'

She moved away to the foot of the bed, talking a little more, in a low voice, half to herself. He saw her screw up her eyes, into crumpled pouches, greyish yellow against the light. You could not tell what suffering had made up her life, or if only time and sun had wrinkled the skin of her face below the stringy hair.

'I am old enough to remember the war of 1870,' she said. She opened the window and emptied the bottle over the sill.

He waited. The bottle seemed to empty very slowly. He heard the splash below.

'As a little girl, in the Paris district, I saw plenty of arms cut off then,' she said. 'Plenty.'

He felt like a small boy; the distance gaping between them was part of history, half the earth. She held the bottle over the sill some time after it had emptied, and did not move. It occurred to him then that she, being so old, might have become happily confused in time, and that she did not even know which war it was. But he was disillusioned.

'I saw plenty in the Great War too,' she said. 'That was butchery.'

What is she trying to tell me? he thought. He watched her give the bottle a final shake, and then she came over again, slowly, to the bed.

'With a sword,' she said, 'that's how they cut them off. I will put the bottle on the table now. So that it will be there when you want it again.'

'I could drink,' he said.

'There is wine and water in the carafe,' she said. 'Can you drink it if I pour it out?' She picked up the carafe and took off its muslin cover. The wine was red, watered down until it was slightly paler than vin rosé. The rosy brightness looked tranquillizing and very cool. 'In the Great War they carted them about like animals: Dear God,' she said, 'Dear God.'

She poured out a little of the wine, the movement casual and meditative, as with the bottle.

'Did you ever hear of the mutiny?'

'Of the French?'

'Of the French,' she said, 'in the Great War. How they rioted at the Gare du Nord and would not go. You have heard of it? And other things?'

'Vaguely,' he said. He raised himself up, with some difficulty, on his right elbow. She stood holding the wine.

'It would be vaguely,' she said. 'It was never in the papers.'

'No,' he said. 'It never is in the papers.' This war was after all the same as others.

She held the glass on his lips and he guided it with his own hand. Movement had drawn the entire strength from his fingers, leaving them like flaky shells of dry flesh. He felt they would crumble to pieces. The wine was cold and a little tart on his lips, and as he swallowed it he discovered how sour his mouth had been.

'That was when France was beaten,' she said. 'Not now. In this war. But then. We were never the same after that.'

The light from the window beat on his eyes. He lowered them and drank again. His strength had practically gone. The last crust of feeling peeled away from his fingers.

'Thank you very much,' he said. 'Thank you.'

'We were no good in this one,' she said, 'because we were butchered in the last. Too many of us were butchered.'

Holding the carafe and the glass, not quite emptied, she stood looking at him and yet past him, inconceivably sad and at the same time not flickering the immeasurably stoical colourless eyes. She shook her head several times and then slowly poured the wine back from the glass into the carafe. 'Yes,' she said. 'Yes. You are very lucky.'

I don't quite see it, he thought. If the Jerries come now I shan't be very lucky. His thoughts were incongruous, but not bitter. The bouncing, slamming beat of blood in his head had gone. But from now on, he thought, I have to get my trousers on with one hand. Why am I lucky?

She set down the carafe on the table, slowly, so that he saw in the movement, like a revelation, bitter and reproachful, all the trial and weariness of her life. She seemed in that moment very, very old. He could not bear the age and anguish of her eyes staring past him, and he knew in another moment why he was lucky. It was because, if the Jerries came, it was not he but they who would suffer. They would take him away and put him safely, somewhere, in a hospital. They would take the rest away, the father, Pierre, the old woman, and the two doctors, and shoot them. They might even, because they liked thoroughness, shoot the horse, too. And they would shoot Françoise.

He remembered her suddenly with alarm. Oh God! he thought, this is a mess. This is the bloodiest mess I ever got myself or anyone else into. Where is she? He looked up to see the old woman walking back across the room, her face not less anguished than the wooden face, dirty with time and blood, of the Christ on the wall. 'Where is Françoise?' he said. For about ten seconds she moved on without speaking. She crossed into the window square of blue sunlight, ready to sit down. Jesus, he thought, Jesus, something has happened. They've done something to her. He felt something greater than his own strength flare up through his body and blow away with its frightened beat all his weakness. Christ Almighty, he thought, if they've done anything to her! 'Where is she, madame?' he said. 'Where is she?'

Reading the Vera Brittain

The second text takes us back to the First World War, or the Great War as the grandmother in the previous text called it. This short, intense poem was written by Vera Brittain for her brother, Captain E.H. Brittain MC, on 11 June 1918; it refers to his wounding two years earlier in the battle of the Somme, and the award of the Military Cross he received for his bravery there. It expresses the hope that he will survive the battles still to come in the war. So, like the previous text, this poem was written while the war in question was still being fought. Vera Brittain was not to know that her brother would be killed just four days after she wrote this poem.

Think about the following issues as you read the poem.

- The language is very simple: how successful is the vocabulary and the **imagery** in conveying the intensity of the author's feelings?
- What does the use of techniques such as **alliteration** and repetition add to the effect of the poem?
- Why do you think the author chose this particular verse form?
- Is this an anti-war poem?

TO MY BROTHER*
(In Memory of July 1st, 1916)

*Captain E. H. Brittain, M.C. Written four days before his death in action in the Austrian offensive on the Italian Front, June 15th, 1918.

Your battle-wounds are scars upon my heart,
   Received when in that grand and tragic 'show'
You played your part
   Two years ago,

And silver in the summer morning sun
   I see the symbol of your courage glow –
That Cross you won
   Two years ago.

Though now again you watch the shrapnel fly,
   And hear the guns that daily louder grow,
As in July
   Two years ago,

May you endure to lead the Last Advance
   And with your men pursue the flying foe
As once in France
   Two years ago.

Vera Brittain

Reading the Lilian M. Anderson

Little is known about Lilian M. Anderson, author of the next poem. Born in Norfolk, she was educated in Torquay and remained in Devon after her marriage, living at Axminster. It is unclear whether *Leave in 1917* is an account of a real person, Sheringham, making an actual journey, or whether it is a product of the poet's imagination. Whatever its origins, it is a text which powerfully evokes the pilot's feelings as he returns to his home county and his young wife, leaving the war temporarily behind him.

It is an unusual poem in that it tells in detail the story of a flight and a railway journey but is at the same time a lyrical and descriptive text. As you read it, think about:

- how the poet continually makes contrasts or comparisons and how these contribute to the mood or effect of the poem
- how the theme of a journey is used as a **metaphor** for Sheringham's state of mind
- why the poet mentions so many place-names
- the effect of the language, particularly unusual words and word-order
- what ideas or attitudes towards war you can find in the poem.

LEAVE IN 1917

Moonlight and death were on the Narrow Seas,
moonlight and death and sleep were on the land:
blindfold the lamps of home, but blinding bright
the wheeling, watching, searching lamps of war.
          To the lone pilot, homing like a dove,
his England was no England. Thought he not
of night-hushed fields and elms, of sleeping farms
where bats, like swallows, hawked about the eaves,
and the white moonlight still as water lay
upon the farmyard and the shippen roofs.
Thought he of hidden forts and hidden camps,
of furnaces down-slaked to darkness, towns
crouched slumbering beneath the threat of death.
   North-west he held till, stooping, he could read
the map-small town of Bedford. Up and on.
Northampton fell behind him. Twenty miles,
and Avon lay, a winding thread of steel,
among its wraith-white meadows.

Low and lower
swept the still wings. Beyond the many roofs,
beyond the chimney-shafts, behind the hills,
the moon hung pallid in an empty sky.
Ached in his throat the scent of morning frost.
The wren-shrill song of every harping wire
was joyful in the silence. Coventry
was yet asleep, but out among the sheds,
new-lit on frosty grass, he found a welcome.

   The crystalled dawn grew red, and the sun crept
above the sharp-rimmed hills. And Sheringham,
seeing the rays smoke white athwart the field,
knew that from dawn to dawn, and once again
from dawn to eve, pain-precious every hour,
lay – God be thanked for it! – two days of leave.

                    ... He travelled south and west.
And still to him his England was no England;
but, rocking to the motion of the train,
half-sleeping where he stood, and sleeping quite
whenever chance and crowds and courtesy
would give him leave to rest, he dreamt of war,
of flights and stunts and crashes; tattered dreams
of month-old happenings.
                    Until at last
his drowsiness was stirred by Devon names –
Exeter, Axminster,
Starcross and Dawlish Warren –
and from his dreams he woke to level waves
that broke on tide-wet shallows.
        Here was his England, stripped of mail and weapons,
child-sweet and maiden-gentle. Here was Spring,
her feet frost-bright among the daffodils.
                    Four months ago
when ice hung from the ferns beside the spring
and robins came for crumbs, had Sheringham,
new-wedded, brought his wife to Devonshire.

The little house stood half-way up the hill,
with milk-white walls, and slated paths that went
like stepping-stones, from April to October,
among a foam of flowers. Apple-trees
leaned from the orchard-slopes; the hillside grass
showed apple-green beneath. Four months ago
had ice hung from the ferns beside the spring:
now, as he climbed the hillside, Sheringham
saw snowdrops in the grass, and heard the lambs
in the Prior's Acre and the valley fields
calling and calling. Clear dripped the spring
beside the orchard-gate.
                    And 'God!' he prayed,
for sunset lay along the upper boughs
of every twisted tree, and emerald dusk
lay stirlessly beneath. And, still as dusk
because she feared to meet her happiness,
his wife stood waiting on the orchard-steeps.
   Love came to them, poor Love, with pinions torn –
poor Love, young Love, that should be auriole-winged.
Scarcely they dared to hold each other close,
young husband and young wife, scarcely to kiss,
lest they should shatter, by their very love,
this rainbow-fragile joy. For every kiss,
however sweet with joy, held lees of tears.
   Like bees that garner sunshine-golden honey
against the barren winter, Sheringham
garnered his memories against the morrow.
Here was the slated threshold of his home,
and here his lighted hearth; here daffodils
shone amber in the firelight; here the breath
of violets and rosy hyacinths
clung heavy to the blue and bitter incense
of lately-kindled logs. And sweet, sweet, sweet
the finches singing in the orchard dusk!

                        Lilian M. Anderson

Reading the Thomas Hardy

The fourth text is an extract from one of Thomas Hardy's less well-known novels, *The Trumpet Major*. This story, set in the time of the Napoleonic Wars, concerns the courting of Anne Garland by three rivals. One is Festus Derriman, a self-opinionated landowner who eventually marries the empty-headed Matilda Johnson. The other two are brothers, John and Bob Loveday, sons of the miller who is landlord to Anne and her mother. John, a serious and sensitive man, is a trumpet major in the British army; Bob is a cheerful, light-hearted sailor. This extract is the last chapter of the novel; Anne has come into a substantial inheritance, but Bob has just heard that his brother's regiment has been ordered overseas to fight. Earlier in the story, it had seemed that Anne would marry John, who loved her deeply; but when he realised Bob also wished to marry her, the trumpet major nobly withdrew from the contest and urged his brother to make the running with Anne.

In reading this extract, think about:

- how the author conveys John's sadness at leaving Anne
- what Hardy says about the quality of soldiers at the time of this story, and what this suggests about his attitudes to society
- the author's feelings about war, revealed in his comments on the fate of the soldiers who said goodbye to Anne
- what effect the final paragraph has on you, and why.

From **The Trumpet Major** *by Thomas Hardy*

John Marches into the Night

During this exciting time John Loveday seldom or never appeared at the mill. With the recall of Bob, in which he had been sole agent, his mission seemed to be complete.

One mid-day, before Anne had made any change in her manner of living on account of her unexpected acquisition, Lieutenant Bob came in rather suddenly. He had been to Budmouth, and announced to the arrested senses of the family that the —th Dragoons were ordered to join Sir Arthur Wellesley in the Peninsula.

These tidings produced a great impression on the household. John had been so long in the neighbourhood, either at camp or in barracks, that they had almost forgotten the possibility of his being sent away; and they now began to reflect upon the singular infrequency of his calls since his brother's return. There was not much time, however, for reflection, if they wished to make the most of John's farewell visit, which was to be paid the same evening, the departure of the regiment being fixed for next day. A hurried valedictory supper was prepared during the afternoon, and shortly afterwards John arrived.

He seemed to be more thoughtful and a trifle paler than of old, but beyond these traces, which might have been due to the natural wear and tear of time, he showed no signs of gloom. On his way through the town that morning a curious little incident had occurred to him. He was walking past one of the churches when a wedding-party came forth, the bride and bridegroom being Matilda and Festus Derriman. At sight of the trumpet-major the yeoman had glared triumphantly; Matilda, on her part, had winked at him slily, as much as to say—. But what she meant heaven knows; the trumpet-major did not trouble himself to think, and passed on without returning the mark of confidence with which she had favoured him.

Soon after John's arrival at the mill several of his friends dropped in for the same purpose of bidding adieu. They were mostly the men who had been entertained there on the occasion of the regiment's advent on the down, when Anne and her mother were coaxed in to grace the party by their superior presence; and the soldiers' well-trained, gallant manners were such as to make them interesting visitors now as at all times. For it was a period when romance had not so greatly faded out of military life as it has done in these days of short service, heterogeneous mixing, and transient campaigns; when the *esprit de corps* was strong, and long experience stamped noteworthy professional characteristics even on rank and file; while the miller's visitors had the additional advantage of being picked men.

They could not stay so long to-night as on that earlier and more cheerful occasion, and the final adieus were spoken at an early hour. It was no mere playing at departure, as when they had gone to Exonbury barracks, and there was a warm and prolonged shaking of hands all round.

'You'll wish the poor fellows good-bye?' said Bob to Anne, who had not come forward for that purpose like the rest. 'They are going away, and would like to have your good word.'

She then shyly advanced, and every man felt that he must make some pretty speech as he shook her by the hand.

'Good-bye! May you remember us as long as it makes 'ee happy, and forget us as soon as it makes 'ee sad,' said Sergeant Brett.

'Good-night! Health, wealth, and long life to 'ee!' said Sergeant-major Wills, taking her hand from Brett.

'I trust to meet 'ee again as the wife of a worthy man,' said Trumpeter Buck.

'We'll drink your health throughout the campaign, and so good-bye t'ee,' said Saddler-sergeant Jones, raising her hand to his lips.

Three others followed with similar remarks, to each of which Anne blushingly replied as well as she could, wishing them a prosperous voyage, easy conquest, and a speedy return.

But, alas, for that! Battles and skirmishes, advances and retreats, fevers and fatigues, told hard on Anne's gallant friends in the coming time. Of the seven upon whom these wishes were bestowed, five, including the trumpet-major, were dead men within the few following years, and their bones left to moulder in the land of their campaigns.

John lingered behind. When the others were outside, expressing a final farewell to his father, Bob, and Mrs. Loveday, he came to Anne, who remained within.

'But I thought you were going to look in again before leaving?' she said gently.

'No; I find I cannot. Good-bye!'

'John,' said Anne, holding his right hand in both hers, 'I must tell you something. You were wise in not taking me at my word that day. I was greatly mistaken about myself. Gratitude is not love, though I wanted to make it so for the time. You don't call me thoughtless for what I did?'

'My dear Anne,' said John, with more gaiety than truthfulness, 'don't let yourself be troubled! What happens is for the best. Soldiers love here to-day and there to-morrow. Who knows that you won't hear of my attentions to some Spanish maid before a month is gone by? 'Tis the way of us, you know; a soldier's heart is not worth a week's purchase—ha, ha! Good-bye, good-bye!'

Anne felt the expediency of his manner, received the affectation as real, and smiled her reply, not knowing that the adieu was for evermore. Then with a tear in his eye he went out of the door, where he bade farewell to the miller, Mrs. Loveday, and Bob, who said at parting, 'It's all right, Jack, my dear fellow. After a coaxing that would have been enough to win three ordinary Englishwomen, five French, and ten Mulotters, she has to-day agreed to bestow her hand upon me at the end of six months. Good-bye, Jack, good-bye!'

The candle held by his father shed its waving light upon John's face and uniform as with a farewell smile he turned on the doorstone, backed by the black night; and in another moment he had plunged into the darkness, the ring of his smart step dying away upon the bridge as he joined his companions-in-arms, and went off to blow his trumpet till silenced for ever upon one of the bloody battle-fields of Spain.

The End

Reading the Anthony Trollope

The final text is a complete short story by Anthony Trollope, who lived from 1815 to 1872. Trollope's best-known work is a series of novels about life in the fictional county of Barsetshire, largely concerned with the role of the church in society. However, despite his success as a writer he was an employee of the Post Office until 1867 which, as he gained promotion, gave him many opportunities to travel within Europe and as far as North and South America, the West Indies and Australia. A number of his short stories have foreign settings, and draw on Trollope's own experiences abroad for the realistic nature of their details.

The idea for this story, *The Two Generals*, which was published in 1863, may have been suggested to Trollope by a meeting he had in America in 1862 with a Senator whose own two sons had fought on opposite sides during the American Civil War; he may also have known Thackeray's novel *The Virginians*, which features two brothers fighting on different sides in the American War of Independence. Like H.E. Bates' *Fair Stood the Wind for France*, and Vera Brittain's poem, this story was published while the war it describes was still in progress, as the opening sentence makes clear.

Despite the maiming suffered by Tom Reckenthorpe, and the passing mention of many thousands of deaths, the focus of the story is more on human relationships than on the horrors of war but, as in the other texts in this chapter, that does not prevent clear ideas and attitudes about warfare emerging through the situations and characters or indeed through the author's own comments.

As you read this story, think about:

- how Trollope presents Major Reckenthorpe and his attempts to deal with the opposing characters and views of his sons
- which of the two brothers you feel more sympathy for, and why; and whether the author appears to favour one brother more than the other
- the character of Ada: do you think Trollope intends her to be admirable, or does he imply any criticism of her behaviour?
- the part played in the story by **irony** (for example, the Reckenthorpe slaves preferring Tom to Frank) and coincidences (for example, the brothers actually coming face to face on the battlefield): to what extent do these features add to, or weaken, the impact of the story?
- the author's attitude to warfare and slavery, particularly his comments in the last paragraph.

by Anthony Trollope

The Two Generals

CHRISTMAS OF 1860 is now three years past, and the civil war which was then being commenced in America is still raging without any apparent sign of an end.[1] The prophets of that time who prophesied the worst never foretold anything so black as this. On that Christmas day, Major Anderson, who then held the command of the forts in Charleston harbour on the part of the United States Government, removed his men and stores from Fort Moultrie to Fort Sumter, thinking that he might hold the one, though not both, against any attack from the people of Charleston, whose state, that of South Carolina, had seceded five days previously. That was in truth the beginning of the war, though at that time Mr Lincoln was not yet President. He became so on the 4th of March, 1861, and on the 15th of April following Fort Sumter was evacuated by Major Anderson, on the part of the United States Government, under fire from the people of Charleston. So little bloody however, was that affair, that no one was killed in the assault; though one poor fellow perished in the saluting fire with which the retreating officer was complimented as he retired with the so-called honours of war. During the three years that have since passed, the combatants have better learned the use of their weapons of war. No one can now laugh at them for their bloodless battles. Never have the shores of any stream been so bathed in blood, as have the shores of those Virginian rivers whose names have lately become familiar to us. None of those old death dooming generals of Europe, whom we have learned to hate for the cold-blooded energy of their trade,—Tilly, Gustavus Adolphus, Frederic, or Napoleon,—none of these ever left so many carcases to the kites as have the Johnsons, Jacksons, and Hookers of the American armies, who come and go so fast that they are almost forgotten before the armies they have led have melted into clay.

Of all the states of the old Union, Virginia has probably suffered the most, but Kentucky has least deserved the suffering which has fallen to her lot. In Kentucky the war has raged hither and thither, every town having been subject to inroads from either army. But she would have been loyal to the Union if she could;—nay,

[1] This story was first published in December 1863.

on the whole she has been loyal. She would have thrown off the plague chain of slavery if the prurient virtue of New England would have allowed her to do so by her own means. But virtuous New England was too proud of her own virtue to be content that the work of abolition should thus pass from her hands. Kentucky, when the war was beginning, desired nothing but to go on in her own course. She wished for no sudden change. She grew no cotton. She produced corn and meat, and was a land flowing with milk and honey. Her slaves were not as the slaves of the Southern States. They were few in number; tolerated for a time because their manumission was understood to be of all questions the most difficult,—rarely or never sold from the estates to which they belonged. When the war broke out Kentucky said that she would be neutral. Neutral, and she lying on the front lines of the contest! Such neutrality was impossible to her,—impossible to any of her children!

Near to the little State capital of Frankfort, there lived at that Christmas time of 1860 an old man, Major Reckenthorpe by name, whose life had been marked by many circumstances which had made him well known throughout Kentucky. He had sat for nearly thirty years in the Congress of the United States at Washington, representing his own State sometimes as Senator and sometimes in the lower house. Though called a major he was by profession a lawyer, and as such had lived successfully. Time had been when friends had thought it possible that he might fill the President's chair; but his name had been too much and too long in men's mouths for that. Who had heard of Lincoln, Pierce, or Polk, two years before they were named as candidates for the Presidency? But Major Reckenthorpe had been known and talked of in Washington longer perhaps than any other living politician.

Upon the whole he had been a good man, serving his country as best he knew how, and adhering honestly to his own political convictions. He had been, and now was, a slave-owner, but had voted in the Congress of his own State for the abolition of slavery in Kentucky. He had been a passionate man, and had lived not without the stain of blood on his hands; for duels had been familiar to him. But he had lived in a time and in a country in which it had been hardly possible for a leading public man not to be familiar with a pistol. He had been known as one whom no man could attack with impunity; but he had also been known as one who would not willingly attack any one. Now, at the time of which I am writing, he was old,—almost on the shelf,—past his duellings and his strong short invectives on the floors of Congress; but he was a man whom no age could tame, and still he was ever talking, thinking, and planning for the political well-being of his State.

In person he was tall, still upright, stiff, and almost ungainly in his gait, with eager grey eyes that the waters of age could not dim, with short, thick, grizzled hair which age had hardly thinned, but which ever looked rough and uncombed, with large hands, which he stretched out with extended fingers when he spoke vehemently;—and of the Major it may be said that he always spoke with vehemence. But now he was slow in his steps, and infirm on his legs. He suffered from rheumatism, sciatica, and other maladies of the old, which no energy of his own could repress. In these days he was a stern, unhappy, all but broken-hearted old man; for he saw that the work of his life had been wasted.

And he had another grief, which at this Christmas of 1860 had already become terrible to him, and which afterwards bowed him with sorrow to the ground. He had two sons, both of whom were then at home with him, having come together under the family roof-tree that they might discuss with their father the political position of their country, and especially the position of Kentucky. South Carolina had already seceded, and other Slave States were talking of secession. What should Kentucky do? So the Major's sons, young men of eight-and-twenty and five-and-twenty, met together at their father's house:— they met and quarrelled deeply, as their father had well known would be the case.

The eldest of these sons was at that time the owner of the slaves and land which his father had formerly possessed and farmed. He was a Southern gentleman, living on the produce of slave labour, and as such had learned to vindicate, if not love, that social system which has produced as its result the war which is still raging at this Christmas of 1863. To him this matter of secession or non-secession was of vital import. He was prepared to declare that the wealth of the South was derived from its agriculture, and that its agriculture could only be supported by its slaves. He went further than this, and declared also, that no further league was possible between a Southern gentleman and a Puritan from New England. His father, he said, was an old man, and might be excused by reason of his age from any active part in the contest that was coming. But for himself there could be but one duty,—that of supporting the new Confederacy, to which he would belong, with all his strength and with whatever wealth was his own.

The second son had been educated at Westpoint, the great military school of the old United States, and was now an officer in the national army. Not on that account need it be supposed that he would, as a matter of course, join himself to the Northern side in the war,—to the side which, as being in possession of the capital and the old Government establishments, might claim to possess a right to his military services. A large proportion of the officers in the pay of the United States leagued themselves with Secession,—and it is difficult to see why such an act would be more disgraceful in them than in others. But with Frank Reckenthorpe such was not the case. He declared that he would be loyal to the Government which he served, and in saying so, seemed to imply that the want of such loyalty in any other person, soldier or non-soldier, would be disgraceful, as in his opinion it would have been disgraceful in himself.

'I can understand your feeling,' said his brother, who was known as Tom Reckenthorpe, 'on the assumption that you think more of being a soldier than of being a man; but not otherwise.'

'Even if I were no soldier, I would not be a rebel,' said Frank.

'How a man can be a rebel for sticking to his own country, I cannot understand,' said Tom.

'Your own country!' said Frank. 'Is it to be Kentucky or South Carolina? And is it to be a republic or a monarchy? Or shall we hear of Emperor Davis? You already belong to the greatest nation on the earth, and you are preparing yourself to belong to the least;—that is, if you should be successful. Luckily for yourself, you have no chance of success.'

'At any rate, I will do my best to fight for it.'

'Nonsense, Tom,' said the old man, who was sitting by.

'It is no nonsense, sir. A man can fight without having been at Westpoint. Whether he can do so after having his spirit drilled and drummed out of him there, I don't know.'

'Tom!' said the old man.

'Don't mind him, father,' said the younger. 'His appetite for fighting will soon be over. Even yet I doubt whether we shall ever see a regiment in arms sent from the Southern States against the Union.'

'Do you?' said Tom. 'If you stick to your colours, as you say you will, your doubts will be soon set at rest. And I'll tell you what, if your regiment is brought into the field, I trust that I may find myself opposite to it. You have chosen to forget that we are brothers, and you shall find that I can forget it also.'

'Tom!' said the father, 'you should not say such words as that; at any rate, in my presence.'

'It is true, sir,' said he. 'A man who speaks as he speaks does not belong to Kentucky, and can be no brother of mine. If I were to meet him face to face, I would as soon shoot him as another;—sooner, because he is a renegade.'

'You are very wicked,—very wicked,' said the old man, rising from his chair,—'very wicked.' And then, leaning on his stick, he left the room.

'Indeed, what he says is true,' said a sweet, soft voice from a sofa in the far corner of the room. 'Tom, you are very wicked to speak to your brother thus. Would you take on yourself the part of Cain?'

'He is more silly than wicked, Ada,' said the soldier. 'He will have no chance of shooting me, or of seeing me shot. He may succeed in getting himself locked up as a rebel; but I doubt whether he'll ever go beyond that.'

'If I ever find myself opposite to you with a pistol in my grasp,' said the elder brother, 'may my right hand——'

But his voice was stopped, and the imprecation remained unuttered. The girl who had spoken rushed from her seat, and put her hand before his mouth.

'Tom,' she said, 'I will never speak to you again if you utter such an oath,—never!'

And her eyes flashed fire at his and made him dumb.

Ada Forster called Mrs Reckenthorpe her aunt, but the connexion between them was not so near as that of aunt and niece. Ada nevertheless lived with the Reckenthorpes, and had done so for the last two years. She was an orphan, and on the death of her father had followed her father's sister-in-law from Maine down to Kentucky;—for Mr Reckenthorpe had come from that farthest and most strait-laced State of the Union, in which people bind themselves by law to drink neither beer, wine, nor spirits, and all go to bed at nine o'clock. But Ada Forster was an heiress, and therefore it was thought well by the elder Reckenthorpes that she should marry one of their sons. Ada Forster was also a beauty, with slim, tall form, very pleasant to the eye; with bright speaking eyes and glossy hair; with ivory teeth of the whitest,—only to be seen now and then when a smile could be won from her; and therefore such a match was thought desirable also by the younger Reckenthorpes. But unfortunately it had been thought desirable by each of them whereas the father and mother had intended Ada for the soldier.

I have not space in this short story to tell how progress had been made in the troubles of this love affair. So it was now, that Ada had consented to become the wife of the elder brother,—of Tom Reckenthorpe, with his home among the slaves,—although she, with all her New England feelings strong about her, hated slavery and all its adjuncts. But when has Love stayed to be guided by any such consideration as that? Tom Reckenthorpe was a handsome, high-spirited, intelligent man. So was his brother Frank. But Tom Reckenthorpe could be soft to a woman, and in that, I think, had he found the means of his success. Frank Reckenthorpe was never soft.

Frank had gone angrily from home when, some three months since, Ada had told him her determination. His brother had been then absent, and they had not met till this their Christmas meeting. Now it had been understood between them, by the intervention of their mother, that they would say nothing to each other as to Ada Forster. The elder had, of course, no cause for saying aught, and Frank was too proud to wish to speak on such a matter before his successful rival. But Frank had not given up the battle. When Ada had made her speech to him, he had told her that he would not take it as conclusive.

'The whole tenor of Tom's life,' he had said to her, 'must be distasteful to you. It is impossible that you should live as the wife of a slave-owner.'

'In a few years there will be no slaves in Kentucky,' she had answered.

'Wait till then,' he had answered; 'and I also will wait.'

And so he had left her, resolving that he would bide his time. He thought that the right still remained to him of seeking Ada's hand, although she had told him that she loved his brother.

'I know that such a marriage would make each of them miserable,' he said to himself over and over again. And now that these terrible times had come upon them, and that he was going one way with the Union, while his brother was going the other way with Secession, he felt more strongly than ever that he might still be successful. The political predilections of American women are as strong as those of American men. And Frank Reckenthorpe knew that all Ada's feelings were as strongly in favour of the Union as his own. Had not she been born and bred in Maine? Was she not ever keen for total abolition, till even the old Major, with all his gallantry for womanhood and all his love for the young girl who had come to his house in his old age, would be driven occasionally by stress of feeling to rebuke her? Frank Reckenthorpe was patient, hopeful, and firm. The time must come when Ada would learn that she could not be a fit wife for his brother.

The time had, he thought, perhaps come already; and so he spoke to her a word or two on the evening of that day on which she had laid her hand upon his brother's mouth.

'Ada,' he had said, 'there are bad times coming to us.'

'Good times, I hope,' she had answered. 'No one could expect that the thing could be done without some struggle. When the struggle has passed we shall say that good times have come.' The thing of which she spoke was that little thing of which she was ever thinking—the enfranchisement of four millions of slaves.

'I fear that there will be bad times first. Of course I am thinking of you now.'

'Bad or good, they will not be worse to me than to others.'

'They would be very bad to you if this State were to secede, and if you were to join your lot to my brother's. In the first place, all your fortune would be lost to him and to you.'

'I do not see that; but of course I will caution him that it may be so. If it alters his views, I shall hold him free to act as he chooses.'

'But, Ada, should it not alter yours?'

'What,—because of my money?—or because Tom could not afford to marry a girl without a fortune?'

'I did not mean that. He might decide that for himself. But your marriage with him under such circumstances as those which he now contemplates, would be as though you married a Spaniard or a Greek adventurer. You would be without country, without home, without fortune, and without standing-ground in the world. Look you, Ada, before you answer. I frankly own that I tell you this because I want you to be my wife, and not his.'

'Never, Frank; I shall never be your wife, whether I marry him or no.'

'All I ask of you now is to pause. This is no time for marrying or for giving in marriage.'

'There I agree with you, but as my word is pledged to him, I shall let him be my adviser in that.'

Late on that same night Ada saw her betrothed and bade him adieu. She bade him adieu with many tears, for he came to tell her that he intended to leave Frankfort very early on the following morning.

'My staying here now is out of the question,' said he. 'I am resolved to secede, whatever the State may do. My father is resolved against secession. It is necessary, therefore, that we should part. I have already left my father and mother, and now

I have come to say good-bye to you.'

'And your brother, Tom?'

'I shall not see my brother again.'

'And is that well after such words as you have spoken to each other? Perhaps it may be that you will never see him again. Do you remember what you threatened?'

'I do remember what I threatened.'

'And did you mean it?'

'No, of course I did not mean it. You, Ada, have heard me speak many angry words, but I do not think that you have known me do many angry things.'

'Never one, Tom:—never. See him then before you go, and tell him so.'

'No,—he is hard as iron, and would take any such telling from me amiss. He must go his way, and I mine.'

'But though you differ as men, Tom, you need not hate each other as brothers.'

'It will be better that we should not meet again. The truth is, Ada, that he always despises any one who does not think as he does. If I offered him my hand he would take it, but while doing so he would let me know that he thought me a fool. Then I should be angry, and threaten him again, and things would be worse. You must not quarrel with me, Ada, if I say that he has all the faults of a Yankee.'

'And the virtues too, sir, while you have all the faults of a Southern ———But, Tom, as you are going from us, I will not scold you. I have, too, a word of business to say to you.'

'And what's the word of business, dear?' said Tom, getting nearer to her, as a lover should do, and taking her hand in his.

'It is this. You and those who think like you are dividing yourselves from your country. As to whether that be right or wrong, I will say nothing now,—nor will I say anything as to your chance of success. But I am told that those who go with the South will not be able to hold property in the North.'

'Did Frank tell you that?'

'Never mind who told me, Tom.'

'And is that to make a difference between you and me?'

'That is just the question that I am asking you. Only you ask me with a reproach in your tone, and I ask you with none in mine. Till we have mutually agreed to break our engagement you shall be my adviser. If you think it better that it should be broken,—better for your own interests, be man enough to say so.'

But Tom Reckenthorpe either did not think so, or else he was not man enough to speak his thoughts. Instead of doing so, he took the girl in his arms and kissed her, and swore that, whether with fortune or no fortune, she should be his, and his only. But still he had to go,—to go now, within an hour or two of the very moment at which they were speaking. They must part, and before parting must make some mutual promise as to their future meeting. Marriage now, as things stood at this Christmas time, could not be thought of even by Tom Reckenthorpe. At last he promised that if he were then alive he would be with her again, at the old family-house at Frankfort, on the next coming Christmas day. So he went, and as he let himself out of the old house, Ada, with her eyes full of tears, took herself up to her bedroom.

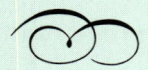

During the year that followed,—the year 1861,—the American war progressed only as a school for fighting. The most memorable action was that of Bull's Run, in which both sides ran away, not from individual cowardice in either set of men, but from that feeling of panic which is engendered by ignorance and inexperience. Men saw wagons rushing hither and thither, and thought that all was lost. After that the year was passed in drilling and in camp-making,—in the making of soldiers, of gunpowder, and of cannons. But of all the articles of war made in that year, the article that seemed easiest of fabrication was a general officer. Generals were made with the greatest rapidity, owing their promotion much more frequently to local interest than to military success. Such a State sent such and such regiments, and therefore must be rewarded by having such and such generals nominated from among its citizens. The wonder, perhaps, is that with armies so formed battles should have been fought so well.

Before the end of 1861, both Major Reckenthorpe's sons had become general officers. That Frank, the soldier, should have been so promoted was, at such a period as this, nothing strange. Though a young man he had been a soldier, or learning the trade of a soldier, for more than ten years, and such service as that might well be counted for much in the sudden construction of an army intended to number seven hundred thousand troops, and which at one time did contain all those soldiers. Frank, too, was a clever fellow, who knew his business, and there were many generals made in those days who understood less of their work that he did. As much could not be said for Tom's quick military advancement. But this could be said for them in the South,—that unless they did make their generals in this way, they would hardly have any generals at all, and General Reckenthorpe, as he so quickly became, General Tom as they used to call him in Kentucky,— recommended himself specially to the Confederate leaders by the warmth and eagerness with which he had come among them. The name of the old man so well known throughout the Union, who had ever loved the South without hating the North, would have been a tower of strength to them. Having him they would have thought that they might have carried the State of Kentucky into open secession. He was now worn-out and old, and could not be expected to take upon his shoulders the crushing burden of a new contest. But his eldest son had come among them eagerly, with his whole heart; and so they made him a general.

The poor old man was in part proud of this and in part grieved.

'I have a son a general in each army,' he said to a stranger who came to his house in those days; 'but what strength is there in a fagot when it is separated? Of what use is a house that is divided against itself? The boys would kill each other if they met.'

'It is very sad,' said the stranger.

'Sad!' said the old man. 'It is as though the devil were let loose upon the earth;—and so he is, so he is.'

The family came to understand that General Tom was with the Confederate army which was confronting the Federal army of the Potomac and defending Richmond; whereas it was well known that Frank was in Kentucky with the army on the Green River, which was hoping to make its way into Tennessee, and which did so early in the following year. It must be understood that Kentucky, though a slave state, had never seceded, and that therefore it was divided off from the Southern States, such as Tennessee and that part of Virginia which had seceded, by a cordon of pickets; so that there was no coming up from the Confederate army to Frankfort, in Kentucky. There could, at any rate, be no easy or safe coming up for such a one as General Tom, seeing that being a soldier he would be regarded as a spy, and certainly treated as a prisoner if found within the northern lines. Nevertheless, General as he was, he kept his engagement with Ada, and made his way into the gardens of his father's house on the night of Christmas-eve. And Ada was the first who knew that he was there. Her ear first caught the sound of his footsteps, and her hand raised for him the latch of the garden door.

'Oh, Tom, it is not you?'

'But it is though, Ada, my darling!' 'Then there was a little pause in his speech. 'Did I not tell you that I should see you to-day?'

'Hush. Do you know who is here? Your brother came across to us from the Green River yesterday.'

'The mischief he did! Then I shall never find my way back again. If you knew what I have gone through for this!'

Ada immediately stepped out through the door and on to the snow, standing close up against him as she whispered to him, 'I don't think Frank would betray you,' she said. 'I don't think he would.'

'I doubt him,—doubt him hugely. But I suppose I must trust him. I got through the pickets close to Cumberland Gap, and I left my horse at Stoneley's half way between this and Lexington. I cannot go back tonight now that I have come so far!'

'Wait, Tom; wait a minute, and I will go in and tell your mother. But you must be hungry. Shall I bring you food?'

'Hungry enough, but I will not eat my father's victuals out here in the snow.'

'Wait a moment, dearest, till I speak to my aunt.'

Then Ada slipped back into the house and soon managed to get Mrs Reckenthorpe away from the room in which the Major and his second son were sitting.

'Tom is here,' she said, 'in the garden. He has encountered all this danger to pay us a visit because it is Christmas. Oh, aunt, what are we to do? He says that Frank would certainly give him up!'

Mrs Reckenthorpe was nearly twenty years younger than her husband, but even with this advantage on her side Ada's tidings were almost too much for her. She, however, at last managed to consult the Major, and he resolved upon appealing to the generosity of his younger son. By this time the Confederate General was warming himself in the kitchen, having declared that his brother might do as he pleased;—he would not skulk away from his father's house in the night.

'Frank,' said the father, as his younger son sat silently thinking of what had been told him, 'it cannot be your duty to be false to your father in his own house.'

'It is not always easy, sir, for a man to see what is his duty. I wish that either he or I had not come here.'

'But he is here; and you, his brother, would not take advantage of his coming to his father's house?' said the old man.

'Do you remember, sir, how he told me last year that if ever he met me on the field he would shoot me like a dog?'

'But, Frank, you know that he is the last man in the world to carry out such a threat. Now he has come here with great danger.'

'And I have come with none; but I do not see that that makes any difference.'

'He has put up with it all that he may see the girl he loves.'

'Psha!' said Frank, rising up from his chair. 'When a man has work to do, he is a fool to give way to play. The girl he loves! Does he not know that it is impossible that she should ever marry him? Father, I ought to insist that he should leave this house as a prisoner. I know that that would be my duty.'

'You would have, sir, to bear my curse.'

'I should not the less have done my duty. But, father, independently of your threat. I will neglect that duty. I cannot bring myself to break your heart and my mother's. But I will not see him. Good-bye, sir. I will go up to the hotel, and will leave the place before daybreak to-morrow.'

After some few further words Frank Reckenthorpe left the house without encountering his brother. He also had not seen Ada Forster since that former Christmas when they had all been together, and he had now left his camp and come across from the army much more with the view of inducing her to acknowledge the hopelessness of her engagement with his brother, than from any domestic idea of passing his Christmas at home. He was a man who would not have interfered with his brother's prospects, as regarded either love or money, if he had thought that in doing so he would in truth have injured his brother. He was a hard man, but one not wilfully unjust. He had satisfied himself that a marriage between Ada and his brother must, if it were practicable, be ruinous to both of them. If this were so, would not it be better for all parties that there should be another arrangement made? North and South were as far divided now as the two poles. All Ada's hopes and feelings were with the North. Could he allow her to be taken as a bride among perishing slaves and ruined whites?

But when the moment for his sudden departure came he knew that it would be better that he should go without seeing her. His brother Tom had made his way to her through cold, and wet, and hunger, and through infinite perils of a kind sterner even than these. Her heart now would be full of softness towards him. So Frank Reckenthorpe left the house without seeing any one but his mother. Ada, as the front door closed behind him, was still standing close by her lover over the kitchen fire, while the slaves of the family with whom Master Tom had always been the favourite, were administering to his little comforts.

Of course General Tom was a hero in the house for the few days that he remained there, and of course the step he had taken was the very one to strengthen for him the affection of the girl whom he had come to see.

North and South were even more bitterly divided now than they had been when the former parting had taken place. There were fewer hopes of reconciliation; more positive certainty of war to the knife; and they who adhered strongly to either side—and those who did not adhere strongly to either side were very few,—held their opinions now with more acrimony than they had then done. The peculiar bitterness of civil war, which adds personal hatred to national enmity, had come upon the minds of the people. And here, in Kentucky, on the borders of the contest, members of the same household were, in many cases, at war with each other.

Ada Forster and her aunt were passionately Northern, while the feelings of the old man had gradually turned themselves to that division in the nation to which he naturally belonged. For months past the matter on which they were all thinking,—the subject which filled their minds morning, noon, and night,—was banished from their lips because it could not be discussed without the bitterness of hostility. But, nevertheless, there was no word of bitterness between Tom Reckenthorpe and Ada Forster. While these few short days lasted it was all love. Where is the woman whom one touch of romance will not soften, though she be ever so impervious to argument? Tom could sit up-stairs with his mother and his betrothed, and tell them stories of the gallantry of the South,—of the sacrifices women were making, and of the deeds men were doing,—and they would listen and smile and caress his hand, and all for a while would be pleasant; while the old Major did not dare to speak before them of his Southern hopes. But down in the parlour, during the two or three long nights which General Tom passed in Frankfort, open secession was discussed between the two men. The old man now had given way altogether. The Yankees, he said, were too bitter for him.

'I wish I had died first; that is all,' he said, 'I wish I had died first. Life is wretched now to a man who can do nothing.'

His son tried to comfort him, saying that secession would certainly be accomplished in twelve months, and that every Slave State would certainly be included in the Southern confederacy. But the Major shook his head. Though he hated the political bitterness of the men whom he called Puritans and Yankees, he knew their strength and acknowledged their power.

'Nothing good can come in my time,' he said; 'not in my time,—not in my time.'

In the middle of the fourth night General Tom took his departure. An old slave arrived with his horse a little before midnight, and he started on his journey.

'Whatever turns up, Ada,' he said, 'you will be true to me.'

'I will; though you are a rebel all the same for that.'

'So was Washington.'

'Washington made a nation;—you are destroying one.'

'We are making another, dear; that's all. But I won't talk secesh to you out here in the cold. Go in, and be good to my father; and remember this, Ada, I'll be here again next Christmas-eve, if I'm alive.'

So he went, and made his journey back to his own camp in safety. He slept at a friend's house during the following day, and on the next night again made his way through the Northern lines back into Virginia. Even at that time there was considerable danger in doing this, although the frontier to be guarded was so extensive. This arose chiefly from the paucity of roads, and the impossibility of getting across the country where no roads existed. But General Tom got safely back to Richmond, and no doubt found that the tedium of his military life had been greatly relieved by his excursion.

Then, after that, came a year of fighting,—and there has since come another year of fighting; of such fighting that we, hearing the accounts from day to day, have hitherto failed to recognise its extent and import. Every now and then we have even spoken of the inaction of this side or of that, as though the drawn battles which have lasted for days, in which men have perished by tens of thousands, could be renewed as might the old German battles, in which an Austrian general would be ever retreating with infinite skill and military efficacy. For constancy, for blood, for hard determination to win at any cost of life or material, history has known no such battles as these. That the South have fought the best as regards skill no man can doubt. As regards pluck and resolution there has not been a pin's choice between them. They have both fought as Englishmen fight when they are equally in earnest. As regard result, it has been almost altogether in favour of the North, because they have so vast a superiority in numbers and material.

General Tom Reckenthorpe remained during the year in Virginia, and was attached to that corps of General Lee's army which was commanded by Stonewall Jackson. It was not probable, therefore, that he would be left without active employment. During the whole year he was fighting, assisting in the wonderful raids that were made by that man whose loss was worse to the Confederates than the loss of Vicksburg or of New Orleans. And General Tom gained for himself mark, name, and glory,—but it was the glory of a soldier rather than of a general. No one looked upon him as the future commander of an army; but men said that if there was a rapid stroke to be stricken, under orders from some more thoughtful head, General Tom was the hand to strike it. Thus he went on making wonderful rides by night, appearing like a warrior ghost leading warrior ghosts in some quiet valley of the Federals, seizing supplies and cutting off cattle, till his name came to be great in the State of Kentucky, and Ada Forster, Yankee though she was, was proud of her rebel lover.

And Frank Reckenthorpe, the other general, made progress also, though it was progress of a different kind. Men did not talk of him so much as they did of Tom; but the War Office at Washington knew that he was useful,—and used him. He remained for a long time attached to the Western army, having been removed from Kentucky to St Louis, in Missouri, and was there when his brother last heard of him.

'I am fighting day and night,' he once said to one who was with him from his own State, 'and, as far as I can learn, Frank is writing day and night. Upon my word, I think that I have best of it.'

It was but a couple of days after this, the time then being about the latter end of September, that Tom Reckenthorpe found himself on horseback at the head of three regiments of cavalry, near the foot of one of those valleys which lead up into the Blue Mountain ridge of Virginia. He was about six miles in advance of Jackson's army, and had pushed forward with the view of intercepting certain Federal supplies which he and others had hoped might be within his reach. He had expected that there would be fighting, but he had hardly expected so much fighting as came that day in his way. He got no supplies. Indeed, he got nothing but blows, and though on that day the Confederates would not admit that they had been worsted, neither could they claim to have done more than hold their own. But General Tom's fighting was on that day brought to an end.

It must be understood that there was no great battle fought on this occasion.

General Reckenthorpe, with about 1500 troopers, had found himself suddenly compelled to attack about double that number of Federal infantry. He did so once, and then a second time, but on each occasion without breaking the lines to which he was opposed; and towards the close of the day he found himself unhorsed, but still unwounded, with no weapon in his hand but his pistol, immediately surrounded by about a dozen of his own men, but so far in advance of the body of his troops as to make it almost impossible that he should find his way back to them.

As the smoke cleared away and he could look about him, he saw that he was close to an uneven, irregular line of Federal soldiers. But there was still a chance, and he had turned for a rush, with his pistol ready for use in his hand, when he found himself confronted by a Federal officer. The pistol was already raised, and his finger was on the trigger, when he saw that the man before him was his brother.

'Your time is come,' said Frank, standing his ground very calmly. He was quite unarmed, and had been separated from his men and ridden over; but hitherto had not been hurt.

'Frank!' said Tom, dropping his pistol arm, 'is that you?'

'And you are not going to do it then?' said Frank.

'Do what?' said Tom, whose calmness was altogether gone. But he had forgotten that threat as soon as it had been uttered, and did not even know to what his brother was alluding.

But Tom Reckenthorpe, in his confusion at meeting his brother, had lost whatever chance there remained to him of escaping. He stood for a moment or two, looking at Frank, and wondering at the coincidence which had brought them together, before he turned to run. Then it was too late. In the hurry and scurry of the affair all but two of his own men had left him, and he saw that a rush of Federal soldiers was coming up around him.

Nevertheless he resolved to start for a run.

'Give me a chance, Frank,' he said, and prepared to run. But as he went,—or rather before he had left the ground on which he was standing before his brother, a shot struck him, and he was disabled. In a minute he was as though he were stunned; then he smiled faintly, and slowly sunk upon the ground.

'It's all up, Frank,' he said, 'and you are in at the death.'

Frank Reckenthorpe was soon kneeling beside his brother, amidst a crowd of his own men.

'Spurrell,' he said to a young officer who was close to him, 'it is my own brother.'

'What, General Tom?' said Spurrell. 'Not dangerously, I hope?'

By this time the wounded man had been able, as it were, to feel himself and to ascertain the amount of the damage done him.

'It's my right leg,' he said; 'just on the knee. If you'll believe me, Frank, I thought it was my heart at first. I don't think much of the wound, but I suppose you won't let me go.'

Of course they wouldn't let him go, and indeed if they had been minded so to do, he could not have gone. The wound was not fatal, as he had at first thought; but neither was it a matter of little consequence as he afterwards asserted. His fighting was over, unless he could fight with a leg amputated between the knee and the hip.

Before nightfall General Tom found himself in his brother's quarters, a prisoner on parole, with his leg all but condemned by the surgeon. The third day after that saw the leg amputated. For three weeks the two brothers remained together, and after that the elder was taken to Washington, — or rather to Alexandria, on the other side of the Potomac, as a prisoner, there to await his chance of exchange. At first the intercourse between the two brothers was cold, guarded, and uncomfortable; but after a while it became more kindly than it had been for many a day. Whether it were cold or kindly, its nature, we may be sure, was such as the younger brother made it. Tom was ready enough to forget all personal animosity as soon as his brother would himself be willing to do so; though he was willing enough also to quarrel,—to quarrel bitterly as ever,—if Frank should give him occasion. As to that threat of the pistol, it had passed away from Tom Reckenthorpe, as all his angry words passed from him. It was clean forgotten. It was not simply that he had not wished to kill his brother, but that such a deed was impossible to him. The threat had been like a curse that means nothing,—which is used by passion as its readiest weapon when passion is impotent. But with Frank Reckenthorpe words meant what they were intented to mean. The threat had rankled in his bosom from the time of its utterance, to that moment when a strange coincidence had given the threatener the power of executing it. The remembrance of it was then strong upon him, and he had expected that his brother would have been as bad as his word. But his brother had spared him; and now, slowly, by degrees, he began to remember that also.

'What are your plans, Tom?' he said, as he sat one day by his brother's bed before the removal of the prisoner to Alexandria.

'Plans?' said Tom. 'How should a poor fellow like me have plans? To eat bread and water in prison at Alexandria, I suppose?'

'They'll let you up to Washington on your parole, I should think. Of course, I can say a word for you.'

'Well, then, do say it. I'd have done as much for you, though I don't like your Yankee politics.'

'Never mind my politics now, Tom.'

'I never did mind them. But at any rate, you see I can't run away.'

It should have been mentioned a little way back in this story that the poor old Major had been gathered to his fathers during the past year. As he had said himself, it would be better for him that he should die. He had lived to see the glory of his country, and had gloried in it. If further glory, or even further gain, were to come out of this terrible war,—as great gains to men and nations do come from contests which are very terrible while they last,—he at least would not live to see it. So when he was left by his sons, he turned his face to the wall and died. There had of course been much said on this subject between the two brothers when they were together, and Frank had declared how special orders had been given to protect the house of the widow, if the waves of the war in Kentucky should surge up around Frankfort. Land very near to Frankfort had become debateable between the two armies, and the question of flying from their house had more than once been mooted between the aunt and her niece; but, so far, that evil day had been staved off, and as yet Frankfort, the little capital of the State, was Northern territory.

'I suppose you will get home,' said Frank, after musing awhile, 'and look after my mother and Ada?'

'If I can I shall, of course. What else can I do with one leg?'

'Nothing in this war, Tom, of course.'

Then there was another pause between them.

'And what will Ada do?' said Frank.

'What will Ada do? Stay at home with my mother.'

'Ay,—yes. But she will not remain always as Ada Forster.'

'Do you mean to ask whether I shall marry her;—because of my one leg? If she will have me, I certainly shall.'

'And will she? Ought you to ask her?'

'If I found her seamed all over with small-pox, with her limbs broken, blind, disfigured by any misfortune which could have visited her, I would take her as my wife all the same. If she were penniless it would make no difference. She shall judge for herself; but I shall expect her to act by me as I would have acted by her.' Then there was another pause. 'Look here, Frank,' continued General Tom, 'if you mean that I am to give her up as a reward to you for being sent home, I will have nothing to do with the bargain.'

'I had intended no such bargain,' said Frank, gloomily.

'Very well; then you can do as you please. If Ada will take me, I shall marry her as soon as she will let me. If my being sent home depends upon that, you will know how to act now.'

Nevertheless he was sent home. There was not another word spoken between the two brothers about Ada Forster. Whether Frank thought that he might still have a chance through want of firmness on the part of the girl; or whether he considered that in keeping his brother away from home he could at least do himself no good; or whether, again, he resolved that he would act by his brother as a brother should act, without reference to Ada Forster, I will not attempt to say. For a day or two after the above conversation he was somewhat sullen, and did not talk freely with his brother. After that he brightened up once more, and before long the two parted on friendly terms. General Frank remained with his command and General Tom was sent to the hospital at Alexandria,— or to such hospitalities as he might be able to enjoy at Washington in his mutilated state,— till that affair of his exchange had been arranged.

In spite of his brother's influence at head-quarters this could not be done in a day; nor could permission be obtained for him to go home to Kentucky till such exchange had been effected. In this way he was kept in terrible suspense for something over two months, and mid-winter was upon him before the joyful news arrived that he was free to go where he liked. The officials in Washington would have sent him back to Richmond had he so pleased, seeing that a Federal general officer, supposed to be of equal weight with himself, had been sent back from some Southern prison in his place; but he declined any such favour, declaring his intention of going home to Kentucky. He was simply warned that no pass South could after this be granted to him, and then he went his way.

Disturbed as was the state of the country, nevertheless railways ran from Washington to Baltimore, from Baltimore to Pittsburgh, from Pittsburgh to

Cincinnati, and from Cincinnati to Frankfort. So that General Tom's journey home, though with but one leg, was made much faster, and with less difficulty, than that last journey by which he reached the old family house. And again he presented himself on Christmas Eve. Ada declared that he remained purposely at Washington, so that he might make good his last promise to the letter: but I am inclined to think that he allowed no such romantic idea as that to detain him among the amenities of Washington.

He arrived again after dark, but on this occasion did not come knocking at the back door. He had fought his fight, had done his share of the battle, and now had reason to be afraid of no one. But again it was Ada who opened the door for him. 'Oh, Tom; oh, my own one!' There never was a word of question between them as to whether that unseemly crutch and still unhealed wound was to make any difference between them. General Tom found before three hours were over that he lacked the courage to suggest that he might not be acceptable to her as a lover with one leg. There are times in which girls throw off all their coyness, and are as bold in their loves as men. Such a time was this with Ada Forster. In the course of another month the elder general simply sent word to the younger that they intended to be married in May, if the war did not prevent them; and the younger general simply sent back word that his duties at head-quarters would prevent his being present at the ceremony.

And they were married in May, though the din of war was going on around them on every side. And from that time to this the din of war is still going on, and they are in the thick of it. The carnage of their battles, and the hatreds of their civil contests, are terrible to us when we think of them; but may it not be that the beneficent power of Heaven, which they acknowledge as we do, is thus cleansing their land from that stain of slavery, to abolish which no human power seemed to be sufficient?

Comparing the texts

Now that you have considered all five texts in this chapter, think about the following points of comparison and contrast between them.

- Which authors are most or least successful in showing how war affects the everyday life of ordinary people? Why?
- Which of the texts is most successful in portraying bravery in the face of hardship and how does the author achieve this success?

- How do the genre qualities of prose and poetry influence the effect different texts have on you?
- What effect does the social and historical setting of each text have on its content and on the ideas, values or attitudes it conveys?
- What does a comparison of the Trollope, Hardy and Bates texts show you about some of the changes in the English language between the mid-nineteenth and mid-twentieth century? Does the language of the Bates now seem old-fashioned in any ways?

Writing about the texts

When you have thought about the texts, look at the following tasks and decide if you would like to write a response to one of them. If you want to use your response as a piece of coursework, remember to check the specific demands of the syllabus you are following with your teacher: for example, you may need to refer to text published before and after 1900 in any piece of coursework you present for assessment, in which case Task 13 would be unsuitable.

Tasks

11. In both *Leave in 1917* and *The Two Generals* the theme of love is as important as the wartime setting. Explore how each author presents this theme, and how the setting is used in each case to give a significant **context** for the human emotions; explain which text succeeds more in conveying strong feelings to you, and why.

12. Judging by the extracts included in this chapter, would you sooner read the complete text of *Fair Stood the Wind for France* or *The Trumpet Major*? In explaining your decision, write about the interest aroused by the characters, setting, ideas and attitudes in the extracts and consider the skill shown by each author in his use of situation and language.

13. *To My Brother* and *Leave in 1917* are very different kinds of poem, but share some themes and ideas. Write about each text, explaining how it conveys its ideas and achieves its effects through the author's use of particular poetic structures and devices. Which poem moves you more, and why?

14. Three of these texts involve brothers, a real person in the case of Vera Brittain's poem and fictional relationships in the Hardy and Trollope stories. How does each of these authors make the relationship important to the ideas he or she is expressing, and how successful is each in describing the strength of feelings involved?

15. What range of attitudes towards war is displayed by all five authors of the texts in this chapter? Consider how these attitudes may have been shaped by the times in which they wrote, or the periods which they describe; how successfully does each writer use content, structure and language to convey their ideas? Are any of the texts more successful than others, and why?

Glossaries

H.E. Bates, Fair Stood the Wind for France

acutely	sharply
anguish	agony
beaucoup	very much
bloodiest	worst
carafe	glass bottle for water or wine
claret	red wine made in Bordeaux
coherent	logical, orderly
corset	strapping
coverlet	bedspread
crumpled	creased
delicacy	politeness
fundamental	basic, everyday
gaping	opening up
Great War	the First World War
immobile	still, unmoving
inconceivably	unimaginably
incongruous	inappropriate
ironic	humorous (because of the strangeness of the situation)
Jerries	Germans
meditatively	thoughtfully
merci	thank you
muslin	thin cotton
realized	carried out
recede	fade away
reproachful	blaming, critical
stoical	resigned, accepting
tart	sharp, bitter
vin rosé	rose (pink) wine

Vera Brittain, To My Brother

Cross	the Military Cross
endure	survive
foe	enemy
grand	large-scale, wonderful (ironic)
'show'	the Battle of the Somme
shrapnel	fragments of shells or bullets
symbol	sign
tragic	pitiable

Lilian M. Anderson, Leave in 1917

athwart	across
auriole	haloed, with a border of brightness
barren	bare, harsh
blindfold	blacked out

crystalled	brilliant, glassy
down-slaked	quenched, put out
eaves	edges of a roof that stick out above a wall
eve	evening, dusk
garner	gather, collect
harping	making a musical sound
hawked	hunted
held	stayed on course
kindled	lighted
lees	sediment
mail	armour
morrow	next day
Narrow Seas	the English Channel
pallid	pale, washed-out
pinions	wings
shallows	water at the edge of a river or the sea
shippen	stable or cowshed
slated	made of slate
steeps	slopes
stunts	daring acts
threshold	doorway
wheeling	circling
wraith-white	ghostly-white

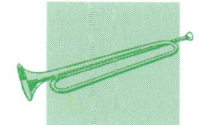

Thomas Hardy, The Trumpet Major

acquisition	gain
adieu	farewell
advent	arrival
affectation	pretended emotion
arrested	interested, captured (attention)
bestowed	presented
conquest	victory
down	hillside
esprit de corps	sense of shared purpose
expediency	appropriateness
fatigues	punishments
forth	out
gallant	polite
heterogeneous	of different types
Mulotters	mulattos, i.e. persons of mixed negro and white parentage
Peninsula	Spain
picked men	commissioned officers
prosperous	comfortable
rank and file	ordinary soldiers (i.e. not officers)
romance	sense of adventure or mystery
singular	remarkable

Sir Arthur Wellesley	the Duke of Wellington
skirmishes	short, quick fights
sole agent	the only person involved
transient	short-lived
trifle	little
valedictory	farewell
yeoman	squire, landowner

Anthony Trollope, The Two Generals

abolition	ending of slavery
acrimony	bad feeling
adhering	keeping
adieu	farewell
adjuncts	things that go with it
alluding	making reference
amenities	facilities
amiss	badly
animosity	bad feeling
ascertain	find out
aught	anything
beneficent	generous
betrothed	engaged, promised in marriage
Cain	Cain murdered his brother (Abel) in the Biblical story
carnage	bloodshed, slaughter
combatants	fighters
conclusive	final
contests	battles
convictions	beliefs
coyness	shyness, reserve
debateable	the object of fighting
din	(unpleasant) noise
dooming	condemning
drilling	practising military manoeuvres
effected	carried out
efficacy	success
Emperor Davis	President of the Confederate States
enfranchisement	freeing
engendered	brought about
fabrication	manufacture
fagot	bundle of sticks
gait	manner of walking
grizzled	streaked with grey
guarded	reserved
hitherto	until now
impervious	unpersuadable
import	importance
imprecation	threat
inducing	persuading

infinite	endless
intercourse	communication
invectives	strongly-worded, bitter or sarcastic speeches
Johnsons…Hookers	generals in the Confederate and Union armies in the American Civil War
league	association, union
lot	fortune, future outlook
maladies	illnesses or infirmities
manumission	freedom (from slavery)
mooted	suggested
musing	thinking, reflecting
mutually	together, both
on the part of	on behalf of
paucity	lack
picket	small number of soldiers positioned to give early warnings of enemy movements
pledged	promised
pluck	courage
predilections	preferences or biases
prurient	unhealthily obsessed with sexual thoughts
rankled	caused irritation
rapidity	speed
rebuke	tell off
renegade	traitor
repress	keep away
reproach	criticism
resolved	decided
sciatica	pain in the back of the leg
seamed	marked
seceded	withdrawn (from the Union)
secesh	secession
skulk	creep
staved off	held off
tedium	boredom
tenor	nature
tidings	news
Tilly…Napoleon	a list of famous generals from the past
to the knife	to the bitter end
ungainly	clumsy
unseemly	unattractive
vehemently	passionately, angrily
victuals	food and drink
vindicate	justify
want	lack
wilfully	intentionally
with impunity	without worrying about the consequences
worsted	defeated
Yankee	someone from the northern states of the USA

Only connect: making your own comparisons

Introduction

This chapter encourages you to investigate further some of your own ideas about the texts presented for study in this book. It suggests how you might think about linking them in different ways to bring out their most important qualities. In some cases, you are invited to include other texts you have read, either in school or in your own time. The idea is for you to think confidently about your reading, and how you respond to it. The **comparative** approach can be used not only to show your understanding of texts, and of what authors are trying to do through their writing, but also to convey to others some of the effects reading has on you.

Different meanings

The texts in this book have been grouped in four chapters around various themes or ideas. But if a number of people read any text, they often respond quite differently to its meaning. For example, look again at Vera Brittain's *To My Brother* (page 93). You could say this is an angry, anti-war poem, with the clear message that wasting young lives in battle makes no sense. Another reader might argue that, on the contrary, it's a quietly courageous poem about her brother's bravery in going to war, and the poet's emotional strength in not stopping him. Neither of these interpretations is right or wrong; the poem can be read in both ways, and you may have other ideas about its meaning as well.

How you respond to a text depends on many factors, including:

- your own attitudes or beliefs (for example, is war always wrong, or is it sometimes necessary?)
- your own experiences (have you ever been in a situation similar to that described in a text, and how did you feel about it or react to it? If not, can you imagine what it might feel like?)
- the situation or mood you happen to be in when you read a text (which may push you towards a cheerful, or more gloomy, personal response)
- the writer's skill (the best writers seldom deliver a simple, straightforward message: they encourage different interpretations, particularly through their use of language and other techniques).

Your reading memory

There is something else which affects your response to a text, and that 'something else' is really the subject of this book. It concerns the understanding you build up over a period of time of all the memorable texts you have read. Or to describe it differently, your own mental 'database' of writers, themes, approaches, situations, and so on. You may not be particularly aware of it, but it's there and it's growing all the time you read. Whenever you respond strongly to a text, it enters that memory bank, which then becomes the basis by which you judge the appeal or effectiveness of new texts that you discover through your own wide reading.

To return to a point made at the start of the Introduction (page 4), we are constantly making comparisons in our daily lives. Most of them are subconscious, that is, they are made without deliberately thinking about them. But when you are asked to compare texts in a GCSE examination, you need to make comparisons by deliberately working through some of the strategies and skills suggested in this book. Drawing on your memory bank of texts can provide you with additional ideas and raw materials which will help you to produce responses of a high standard.

Planning points

If you have successfully worked through the discussion points and some of the tasks suggested in previous chapters, or any other material provided by your teacher, you should be clear about the two starting-points in comparing texts, which are really the same as in any other aspect of examination preparation:

- what are the GCSE examiners looking for?

and

- how do you provide it for them?

In this case, the examiners are looking for your ability to show the reading skills described in pages 5–6 of the Introduction through close and detailed knowledge of a range of texts.

Once you are fully aware of the purpose of this part of your GCSE course, you can think about constructing your own comparative reading tasks. There are three ways of setting about this. You can:

- use texts in this book, but link them differently to bring out points of comparison or contrast which have occurred to you in the course of reading them,

or you could:

- introduce some texts which you have found yourself and which provide interesting comparisons or contrasts with texts in this book.

If you have read widely, you might be able to:

- use texts entirely of your own choice, linking them by theme, genre or technique in ways similar to those suggested in Chapters 1–4.

Whichever approach you take, and before you start planning your own comparative tasks, look back at pages 5–7 of the Introduction. Think again about the importance of:

- assessment objectives (that is, the skills which GCSE examiners are looking to credit and reward in your work), and
- the questions raised in the *How do I get started?* section (page 7).

You must also remember to make sure that you understand what your particular GCSE syllabus is asking for: check these points with your teacher so that you don't put a lot of effort into something which cannot be used in your coursework or which will not be tested in your examination papers.

Make sure as well that you really understand the words used in tasks and words which you will be expected to use in your responses: check the glossary at the end of this book if you are not sure.

New tasks, new texts

To help you get started, here are some sample tasks which take all three approaches suggested above. The first two link texts from different chapters of this book by identifying similarities in theme or technique; Task 16 chooses the texts for you, but Task 17 allows your own choice of texts.

16 Texts:
   A Trampwoman's Tragedy (Hardy, pages 31–4) and *Leave in 1917* (Anderson, pages 94–6)

   Both texts are poems which describe journeys, and in which real places are significant. However, they are quite different in theme, structure and language. Write about the effects achieved by the authors, and how the language and structure of the poems helps in this. Which poem do you feel is more successful, and why?

17 Texts:
   either *Mrs. Turner Cutting the Grass* (Shields, pages 8–14) **or** *The Outside Dog* (Bennett, pages 61–8)
   and *Silas Marner* (Eliot, pages 75–82) **or** *The Trumpet Major* (Hardy, pages 97–99)

   In both texts, the reader has a better understanding of the situations than the main characters themselves. Write about how each author achieves this effect, and how this affects your response to the characters' situations and to each author's attitudes and concerns. Refer to details of language and structure to support your argument.

The next two tasks suggest how you can introduce additional texts to provide contrast or comparison with some of the texts in this book. You could use these tasks as models for creating some of your own, using different texts from this book and others that you have read for yourself.

18 Texts:
   Spoonface Steinberg (Hall, pages 83–5) and a deathbed scene from a nineteenth-century novel, for example, by Dickens or one of the Bronte sisters

   Write about how each author treats the subject of death and how she or he uses situation, character and language to involve your emotions. Comment on how the social and historical setting of each text affects the author's attitudes and the reader's response, and how radio scripts and novels are able to achieve different effects on the reader.

19 Texts:
   The Two Generals (Trollope, pages 101–20) and a modern short story which deals with disagreement between family members in another culture or tradition (for example, by Bernard MacLaverty, Farrukh Dhondy or Margaret Atwood)

Write about how successfully each author presents the disagreement and how she or he uses language and structure to reflect the seriousness of the situation and to engage your sympathies with the characters. Comment on how the setting of each text influences the author's approach.

The final task is completely open, and can be applied to almost any combination of texts, but you will need to think carefully about giving it a clear focus and purpose: remember that you can't write about every aspect of long or thought-provoking texts in the space of a few pages. Always think about what it is you want to show (refer to the assessment objectives on page 6 again if you are unsure), and concentrate on doing that in detail, using those parts of the text which are most relevant to your argument.

20 Texts:

any two or three of your own choice – but if this is intended to be a piece of GCSE coursework make sure that you check with your teacher about the particular demands of your GCSE syllabus, which may restrict your choice of author, period or genre

Compare how the authors use situation, language and structure to convey their ideas powerfully to the reader. Which of them is most successful, and why?

Tasks 16–20 in this chapter, as well as those in earlier chapters, provide you with models which you can adapt for writing about different themes or different texts – and if you have other ideas of your own, so much the better! Discuss them with your teacher, who will be able to suggest alternative approaches, additional texts, and ways of planning – especially how to make sure that you respond in sufficient detail and don't over-generalise.

6 Students' work: responses to comparative reading

Introduction

This chapter comprises several brief extracts from actual GCSE students' writing which compares texts. These extracts have been chosen to show certain approaches in action, but also as an opportunity to point out how the response is already of a good standard, or how it might have been improved. The texts used are not included in this book, but you should still be able to appreciate the skills shown by the students in writing about them. You might like to obtain copies of the texts for yourself if you think they sound interesting – one or more of them could certainly be used in some of the tasks suggested in Chapter 5.

Student 1

Here is the opening of an essay which compares two texts:

> I have chosen to study 'The Red Room', a pre-twentieth century story, and 'The Man Who Didn't Believe in Ghosts', a twentieth century piece of writing. Both are similar in terms of genre and theme (short stories about ghosts), but the two authors have used two very different styles of writing. I will be comparing these two stories in my essay.

This is a confident, clear beginning. The student shows that he:

- understands the theme of the texts
- has thought about how the writers use language
- is aware of how the choice of a particular form or genre (in this case, a ghost story) may be used to create certain effects on the reader.

He also suggests an awareness of how the historical period in which a text is written or set may influence the writer's style or the reader's response.

This is only the beginning – the student hasn't come to the main part of the essay yet, so there is no detail about the texts – but it sets out a clear structure for the essay (genre, theme, language) within which the candidate will be able to explain fully his response to these two stories.

Student 2

Endings of essays which compare texts are just as important as the beginnings. You need to leave your reader with a brief summary of what the comparison has achieved; in other words, what you have learned about the texts (or about reading in general) from completing the assignment.

The next student has compared two detective stories, *The Speckled Band* by Sir Arthur Conan Doyle (a short story about the detective, Sherlock Holmes) and *Seeing is Believing*, a novel by Elizabeth Ferrars. This is how she ends her essay:

> In 'Seeing is Believing' there is a series of past murders, one main present murder not connected with the others and some blackmailing. In Sherlock Holmes the way the crimes have been committed is the most unique part, but with 'Seeing is Believing' it is why the murders have been committed is the most unusual part. This is the same for most modern detective stories; the detectives are looking for the motives of the crimes. Modern detective writers look at the psychological meaning behind the crimes rather than the way the crimes are carried out.

The main point is good, although it is not expressed very clearly. It shows that this student has gone further than the one previously quoted in understanding the importance of the historical period in which the two texts were written. She explains how this has influenced the authors' different approaches to writing as well as the reader's response and so has contrasted an important aspect of two texts which have the obvious similarity of both being detective stories.

It is a rather abrupt ending, however. The student doesn't sum up her personal response by stating which of the stories is more interesting, or more successful; she doesn't explain what the main themes are, or how a short story is different from a novel and what effect this has on the author's methods. She doesn't really tell us what she has learned about the two writers' skills from carrying out the comparison. A couple of extra sentences on the end would have made all the difference; something like this, perhaps:

> I preferred 'Seeing is Believing', because I enjoyed getting inside the mind of the criminal and realising that quite ordinary people may be capable of terrible acts. The characters in the Sherlock Holmes story were less important than the solution to the mystery, and because it is only a short story the characters could not be as developed as those in the Ferrars novel.

The additional sentences round off the essay neatly by summarising the student's opinions about the texts and the new understanding she has gained from them, and show some awareness of how short stories may differ from novels in at least one respect.

Student 3

The major part of any comparative essay must look in detail at aspects of texts such as situation or setting, character and language, as well as the themes or ideas put forward by the authors. Here is another student writing about the same Sherlock Holmes story, *The Speckled Band*, but comparing it this time with an American short story, *Full Circle* by Sue Grafton. The student comments on different uses of language in the two texts:

> Arthur Conan Doyle's 'The Speckled Band' is very old fashioned; speech is formal and the order of words is different to modern day. Instead of saying 'Did it for love not money', Conan Doyle has written 'For working as he did rather for love of his art than for the acquirement of wealth'. Slang is very common in 'Full Circle', such as 'There's gotta be a way to track him down, don't you think?'

The extract shows the importance of making references to texts through direct, well-chosen quotation. However, a top-grade student would go further than just making general comments, as this essay does. He or she might look at how the language used by different characters, or the language used to describe actions or situations as opposed to pure description, varies *within* each text as well as *between* them. Nineteenth-century writers do use slang, and twentieth-century writers do sometimes use a very formal style, although the student quoted above implies that this is not so. Good GCSE students will look beyond the obvious, surface features of texts and speculate why, and to what effect, writers have chosen particular methods, techniques or language.

Student 4

Another indication of a top-grade essay is when a student shows the ability to extract and explain different ideas or implications which lie beneath the surface meaning of texts. In the following extract, the student is comparing a poem by Moniza Alvi, *Presents from My Aunts in Pakistan* with a short story by Tayeb Salih, *A Handful of Dates*. She sees and explains the similarity in theme within these texts, and uses detail from both texts to illustrate it:

> The point of view, moral or message that the writers are trying to say is that even though the values and customs are passed down through generations, elders should be aware of the conflict that this can cause. Future generations should be left free to explore other religions and cultures without feeling oppressed, as this can have a damaging effect on the emotional and social development of the child, resulting in confusion or rebellion. Also the grandfather should practise what his religion preaches. It is no good praying to Allah five times a day and reciting from the Koran then carrying out acts that are sinful. The aunts in the poem send the girl traditional clothing, yet wish themselves for cardigans from Marks and Spencer.

This student goes on to explain how writers use the possibilities of different genres, in this case a poem and a short story, to create particular effects, in this case the immediacy of the poem contrasted with the slower build-up in the story:

> Although both texts are written in the first person and so speak directly to the reader, the story uses descriptions of characters and scenery to tell the narrative, whereas the shorter poem only describes objects and items and leaves the reader to fill in the character of the speaker. A lot of dashes and short sentences are used as if the girl is pausing to gather her thoughts before she makes another statement. Each verse changes according to the girl's thoughts. We see a contrast in the writing in the story as the grandfather speaks to the boy and gradually changes the mood from a description of the idyllic surroundings he lives in to one of revenge.

This student could have explained more fully that a short story allows for deliberate changes in **pace** or **atmosphere**, while a poem is (usually) shorter and so depends more on either developing one idea or, as in this case, moving swiftly from one mood to another using words and punctuation economically. Nevertheless, this is a good example of an able student using detail to convey both her personal response to *what* the texts are about and her critical understanding of *how* the writers achieve the effects that she describes.

And finally…

…remember that memory bank of reading mentioned in Chapter 5: keep searching for texts which say something new to you, or say something in a new way. Keep searching for that sense of excitement when you:

- make connections between apparently different texts
- realise that a text has cast new light on the world in which you live
- discover ideas in texts which challenge and involve you.

If you do this, and can pass on your understanding to other readers, you will not only do well in your GCSE examinations but, more importantly, will have discovered the power of books to develop your own critical thinking and illuminate your life.

Glossary of technical terms

Introduction

The terms explained here are all used in this book and are part of the common language of critical writing. You need to know their meaning so that you can understand them when they are used by others, and so that you can use them yourself in order to explain precisely what you mean when talking or writing about texts. This is not a complete list of words that you might need to know – look out for other technical terms, and make sure that you find out their meanings. The definitions given here apply to the words as used in the context of this book – they may have other meanings in different circumstances!

action	what takes place in a text, for example, what a **character** in a story does, what a **poem** describes or what a play dramatises
alliteration	repetition of a sound, usually at the beginnings of words; used to draw attention to, or to highlight, an idea or event; often used in conjunction with **onomatopoeia**
approach	the way a writer presents his or her **subject-matter**, for example, in a serious or lighthearted way; see also **attitude** and **tone**
archaic	old-fashioned or no longer used; writers sometimes use archaic words if they are setting a text in a previous age and wish to create an illusion of authenticity
assessment objectives	the skills on which you are tested in an examination; see Chapter 1 of this book for a full discussion of this topic
assignment	another word for an examination question or **task**, most often applied to a coursework task which requires reading and research
atmosphere	the feeling or mood created by a writer, for example, fear in a ghost story or happiness in a love poem
attitude	similar to **approach**, that is, how a writer feels about his or her **subject-matter**
audience	the readership at which a text is directed, for example, children or adults
autobiography	someone's life-story written by the person him or herself; this may be a real or a fictional person
ballad	a **poem** which tells a story, usually in short rhyming verses with frequent **repetition** of words or lines; originally written for oral performance rather than silent reading

body language	sometimes referred to as 'non-verbal communication' in other words, what you can tell about someone's mood or frame of mind by the expression on their face, the way they are standing or sitting, etc.
character	a person in a literary text
chronological	arranged in the order of occurrence; so a story may be chronological, in which case it relates events in the sequence they occurred; or it may involve **flashbacks** which disturb the actual order of events
coincidence	an apparently chance or unlikely event which creates an unexpected and significant **situation**, for example when the Cook in the Wilkie Collins story finds herself in the same house as the man who jilted her
comedy	light-hearted or amusing events
comparative	comparative writing explores how two or more texts are similar or different and how this helps to explain both their meaning and their relative success
content	what a literary text is about; the story of a novel, or the idea behind a poem, for example
context	see **setting**
culture	a **society** at a particular time, which has shared beliefs or **values**, for example, the inhabitants of the southern states of the USA in the time of Trollope's story saw nothing wrong with slavery, while the inhabitants of the northern states wished to end the practice
device	another word for an aspect of an author's **technique** or a stylistic feature, for example **alliteration** or **dramatic irony**
dialect	**language** spoken in a particular geographical area or by a particular group of people, with a vocabulary and grammar of its own
drama	the literary **genre** which describes texts written for performance on stage, or on radio or television
dramatic irony	when the reader, listener or viewer understands more of what is going on than the **characters** involved; for example, you probably realised that Marjory's husband was a murderer in *The Outside Dog* before she does
effect	what you feel when you read a text; this covers your reaction to the **subject-matter** or **ideas** as well as how you feel about particular aspects of a text such as the author's **style**, or the actions of the **characters**

features	the most significant aspects of a text or of a writer's **style**; what it is that makes it different from other texts you have read; also, specific aspects of different **genres**
fiction	an invented story
flashback	a **technique** used to recall an earlier event at a later stage in the story, for example in *Mrs. Turner Cutting the Grass*; used by authors to create a more interesting **structure** in a story than a straightforward **chronological** approach
focus	a clear approach to a **task** which concentrates on the important issues and does not wander off into irrelevancies
form	often used to mean the same as either **genre** or **structure**
frame	a **device** which puts a story within a particular **context** or **setting**; for example, the Collins text in this book, where the beginning and end of the text are set in the present, while the story itself is told as a memory of past events
genre	a **form** or category of literary text, for example, **prose**, **poetry** and **drama**; these may be further subdivided, for example, prose into **short stories** and **novels**, poetry into **ballads** and **lyrics**. Different genres often make use of particular **literary conventions** or **traditions**, and you should try to identify these when writing about texts, particularly if you are comparing different genres
idea	the author's starting point for a text and part of its **theme** or **message**
imagery	descriptive language used in literary texts, for example **similes** or **metaphors**
impact	the strength of effect that a literary text has on you
implicit meaning	what you can work out or deduce beneath the **surface meaning** of a text, for example the depth of Silas Marner's feelings for Eppie even though he says very little when Godfrey and Nancy offer her the chance to live with them
irony	the difference between how you might expect something to be and how it actually is, for example when the slaves in *The Two Generals* like the brother who believes in slavery more than the one who would set them free
language	words chosen by authors to convey their **ideas**, **attitudes** and points of view and to guide our reactions to texts
literary convention	a traditional rule or practice, for example, the features of the **ballad** form described above

literary tradition	similar to **literary convention**, that is, the use of accepted **forms** or **structures** such as verse forms, **rhythm** and **rhyme** in **poetry**, and lifelike **characters** in **fiction**
lyric	a short **poem** which expresses the writer's personal feelings or thoughts
message	what an author wishes his or her **audience** to take as the text's meaning
metaphor	when a word or phrase is applied to something it does not literally resemble in order to emphasise particular qualities, for example 'She was a star'
monologue	a **drama** script for one performer only
multiple viewpoint	when a text gives you a number of accounts of the same situation or person by different **characters** so that you can piece together a fuller understanding of what is going on
narrative	an account or story
narrator	the person who tells the story in the text; it may be told directly by the author (which is known as 'third person' **narrative**) or it may be told through the mouth of one or more of the characters involved (which is known as first person' **narrative**)
novel	a long **prose fiction** text involving **character** and **action** and telling a story; the author's **purpose** is often to convey a particular **idea** or **message** about a **culture** or **society**
onomatopoeia	words whose sound imitates the object or action described, for example 'the murmuring of innumerable bees'; often combined with **alliteration**
optimistic	cheerful, expecting things to turn out for the best
pace	the 'speed' at which a text moves; for example, an adventure story may be 'fast-moving' with lots of incident and dialogue, while a romantic novel may be 'slower', containing less action and more description
pessimistic	gloomy, expecting the worst
plot	the storyline or plan of a **narrative** text
'poetic' language	forms of words which are used in **poetry**, but not in everyday speech, sometimes because they sound pleasanter or fit rhythms more easily, for example 'ne'er' instead of 'never'
poetry	texts in **rhythmic** form, often employing **rhyme** and usually shorter and more concentrated in **language** and **ideas** than either **prose** or **drama**

propaganda	one-sided information intended either to support or threaten a political or military group
prose	text which does not have the rhythmic qualities of **poetry** and which tends to be less concentrated in **language** or **ideas**
purpose	why an author writes a text; the **ideas**, **themes** or **message** he or she wishes to convey to readers
quotation	an actual passage from a text used to support a point made in a critical essay
radio script	a dramatic text written for performance on radio
reference	mention or description of something in a text without using direct **quotation**
repetition	a **device** used by writers to create a particular **effect**; it may be of single letters or sounds, as in **alliteration** and **onomatopoeia**, or it may be of whole words or phrases to create an **atmosphere** or mood as in *A Trampwoman's Tragedy*
response	what you, the reader, feel when you read a text and what you must be able to explain and illustrate in examination answers or coursework
rhyme	words which have the same end-sounds; often used as a **genre feature** of **poetry**
rhythm	the pattern of words formed by long and short sounds or syllables; a **genre feature** of **poetry**
sentimental	something which appeals excessively to your emotions, for example a story in which a perfect child dies of a terrible disease, which brings its previously warring parents together again, only for one of them to die as well
setting	the surroundings or background against which the events described in a text take place; the setting or **context** may be important to the **theme** or **message** of the story, for example in the Trollope text in this book
short story	a **genre** or **form** of **prose fiction**; shorter than a **novel**, and normally dealing with fewer **characters** and less **action**
simile	a **device** which compares one thing directly to another, for example 'Oh, what a sight is Mrs Turner cutting her grass and how, like an ornament, she shines'
situation	a moment or event of significance in a text, for example when a **character** has to make a choice, such as the policeman in the Collins story destroying the letter from the cook

skills	what you need to show in your examination and coursework; see **assessment objectives**
society	the social, historical and cultural background against which texts are set and which influence the **attitudes** or **values** displayed by **characters**; part of an author's **message** is often a comment on the society portrayed in the text, for example in the Shields and Trollope stories in this book
structure	how a literary text is planned and put together, for example, the **form** of verse chosen in a **poem**, the use of a **chronological** approach or **flashbacks** in **prose**, the use of **dramatic irony** in a playscript
style	the choices of **language, literary conventions** and **devices** used by an author in a text; some authors have a very individual, recognisable style
subject-matter	what a text is about; the **attitudes, ideas** and **message** the author wishes his or her **audience** to consider
surface meaning	what the words on the page mean; sometimes, that is all they do mean, but sometimes there are **implicit meanings** too
syllabus	the document published by an examination board which details what you must study and how you will be tested for a qualification such as GCSE
sympathy	the feelings you have towards an author or his or her **characters** when reading a text; skilful authors direct or manipulate your sympathies through their choice and use of **structure, language** and **ideas**
task	another word for **assignment**; a piece of examination or coursework
technique	an author's ability to use **structure, language** and **ideas** to convey his or her **message** clearly to you
theme	another word for **idea** or **message**; what a text is about
tone	the quality or overall **effect** of a text, for example, humorous or serious; **optimistic** or **pessimistic**
values	the moral principals or standards of a person or group of people; literary texts often describe conflicts over values, for example, the Shields and Eliot texts in this book
voiceover	a **device** sometimes used in film or television productions to give the **audience** information which cannot easily be dramatised, such as the thoughts of a **character** or the passage of a long period of time

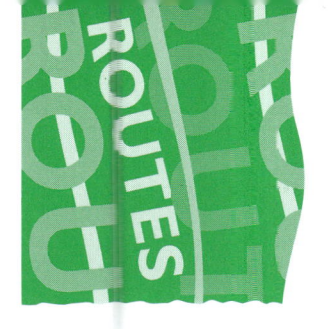

Acknowledgements

The author and publishers wish to thank the following for permission to use copyright material:

BBC Worldwide Ltd for material from Alan Bennett, 'The Outside Dog' from *Talking Heads II* (1998) pp. 60–9. Copyright © Alan Bennett; and Lee Hall, 'Spoonface Steinberg' from *Spoonface Steinberg and Other Plays* (1997) pp. 156–9. Copyright © Lee Hall; Blake Friedmann Literary Agency on behalf of the author for material from Carol Shields, 'Mrs. Turner Cutting the Grass' from *Various Miracles* (1994) Fourth Estate Ltd; Bloomsbury Publishing Plc for material from Michael Ondaatje, *The English Patient* (1992) pp. 3–6; Mark Bostridge and Rebecca Williams, Literary Executors of the Estate of the author, for Vera Brittain, 'To My Brother'; Carcanet Press Ltd for Gillian Clarke, 'Shearing' from *Collected Poems*; Peters Fraser & Dunlop Group Ltd on behalf of the Estate of the author for Laurie Lee, 'The Armoured Valley' from *Selected Poems* by Laurie Lee (1983) Penguin Books; Laurence Pollinger Ltd on behalf of the Estate of the author for material from H. E. Bates, *Fair Stood the Wind for France*, pp. 113–8; A. P. Watt Ltd on behalf of the Literary Executors of the Estate of the author for H. G. Wells, 'The Purple Pileus'.

Every effort has been made to trace the copyright holders but if any have been inadvertently overlooked the publishers will be pleased to make the necessary arrangement at the first opportunity.